SHOW
YOUR
COLORS

SHOW YOUR COLORS

30 Flexible Beading Wire Jewelry Projects

Jamie Hogsett &
Sara Hardin Oehler

KALMBACH BOOKS

We would like to dedicate this book to Mike Sherman and Scott Clark, two of our favorite people and owners of Soft Flex® Company. Without their constant encouragement, support, and innovative products, this project would not have been possible. As a tribute to Mike and Scott, we've named each project after the songs, movies, and trivia of their favorite singer, Cher.

Kalmbach Books
21027 Crossroads Circle
Waukesha, Wisconsin 53186
www.Kalmbach.com/Books

Published in 2012
16 15 14 13 12   1 2 3 4 5

Manufactured in the United States of America

ISBN: 978-0-87116-711-8

Editor *Karin Van Voorhees*
Art Director *Lisa Bergman*
Proofreader *Erica Swanson*
Photographers *William Zuback and James Forbes*

Publisher's Cataloging-in-Publication Data
Hogsett, Jamie, 1978-
  Show your colors : 30 flexible beading wire jewelry projects / Jamie Hogsett & Sara Hardin Oehler.

    p. : chiefly col. ill. ; cm.

    ISBN: 978-0-87116-711-8

    1. Beadwork—Handbooks, manuals, etc. 2. Beadwork—Patterns. 3. Wire jewelry—Handbooks, manuals, etc. 4. Wire jewelry—Patterns. 5. Jewelry making. I. Oehler, Sara Hardin. II. Title.

TT860 .H65 2012
745.594/2

Foreword

Colorful and flexible beading wire opens many doors when used in a jewelry design. If you've picked up this book to enhance your library, or to learn a new technique, I promise it will deliver tenfold. Sara and Jamie create fun jewelry—I adore all of their designs, and always find them inspiring!

I remember my first experience with colorful beading wire. I had endless ideas of how to use this product that both complemented the beads and also held its own in a design. Color can be your best inspiration!

Jamie and Sara have put together 30 colorful jewelry projects that will inspire your own design creativity. Not only that, but they also have compiled an educational introduction that teaches all the basics like understanding wire gauge and what tools to use. This section includes an analysis of different color palettes—a major stepping stone covered in the beginning of the book!

Dark Lady (page 26) is one of my favorite projects. It features a technique I have already tried out myself—anchor beads onto the beading wire by passing the wire through the beads twice. This technique creates a nice detail that shows off the color of the wire. I also love Malibu (page 81), a bangle project that incorporates one of my favorite color palettes. Currently, bangles are quite popular and the versatility of this project has me dreaming up all sorts of design ideas.

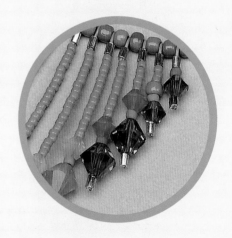

They couldn't have made it any easier for you to get started using color in your jewelry designs! The projects represent a wide range of experience levels—every jewelry fanatic will find a project that suits her taste and ability.

Sara and Jamie have made me look at using wire in a new and exciting way. I know that you'll be equally amazed at all of the possibilities. Be inspired and show your best colors!

—Lorelei Eurto

Lorelei Eurto writes a popular jewelry blog, lorelei1141.blogspot.com, shares her tutorials in many books and magazines, and is the author of *Bohemian Inspired Jewelry: 50 Designs Using Leather Ribbon and Cording*, 2012.

Lots of color inside!

Color makes you feel good!

Whether you are just beginning or you've been at this hobby for a while, you may have seen colored beading wire and are curious about how to incorporate it into your jewelry designs. As beaders, we are accustomed to covering up beading wire with beads. In *Show Your Colors*, we'll teach you how to use colored beading wire as a design element and leave it showing in your bright and fun beaded jewelry.

We are excited to present this collection of 30 brand-new bracelet, necklace, and earrings projects, each with step-by-step photos and instructions. To get you started, we begin with all the basic techniques used in the book, as well as a little bit of information about every product and tool. This overview will help to kick-start your colored beading wire adventure.

The project chapters are organized by technique. We begin with stringing projects featuring small bursts of colored wire and wire wrapped around beads to add texture. Next, you'll find projects that take illusion-style jewelry one (or more!) step further. Knitting spool projects follow; but they're not as challenging as they may appear! Next, we teach you to become a colored beading wire sculptor, and how to create different shapes with beading wire. And finally, you learn how to make intricate-looking jewelry with simple braiding and weaving techniques.

Every project has a general materials and tools list to let you know just what you need to complete the piece. You'll see colored dots at the top of the list that represent each color of wire used in the project, but feel free to experiment with your own! We've included specific sources at the back of the book for some of the harder-to-find components. You will see a lot of crystals and seed beads in these designs (and even a few with no beads at all). Although we did use some specialized beads or findings, we were careful to make sure the bulk of the items used in this book can be easily found at your local bead store, regional bead shows, or favorite online retailers. You should be able to get supplies for almost every project easily, no matter where you live.

Although we hope that you will enjoy our color combinations, we encourage you to consider trying different colors of beading wire and beads when recreating these projects. Use your imagination to make the designs your own! Color can be a reflection of your personality and/or your mood, so look down deep inside and find color combinations that please you and your individual spirit. To help you in that search, we are proud to offer a special contribution from Margie Deeb, renowned color expert and jewelry maker, about choosing pleasing color combinations called *Color Your Emotions*.

More than anything, our hope is that *Show Your Colors* inspires you to have fun and try something new. You will be amazed by the flood of new ideas that pop into your head when colored beading wire becomes a featured ingredient in your designs rather than just a necessary staple.

Sara Oehler   Jamie Hogsett

EVERYTHING YOU NEED TO KNOW

Whether you are new to beading with colored wire or an advanced pro, these basics will teach you everything you need to know about the wire, findings, beads, and tools used in this book.

Color Your Emotions

With colored wire, you're able to add another layer of color and beauty to your jewelry. The beads are no longer the only focal point. You can now go wild splashing bracelets with braids, twists, loops, and tangles of color. You can let whispers of color peek out from between rows of beads, or you can the allow wire to take center stage carrying all the color, while a lone bead plays the supporting role. There are countless ways to let color sing through your jewelry.

So many options can mean free-wheeling fun. But too many options can also overwhelm and intimidate. Just as you're not going to eat every pastry in the bakery (at least not in one sitting), you're not going to use every color available in the same piece of jewelry.

You need a clearly defined focus to help you choose which colors to use and which to set aside.

Think "statement". Ask "what kind of emotional statement do I want this piece of jewelry to convey?" Bold? Playful? Dramatic? Serene? Elegant? Color sets the tone for every statement. And a consciously defined statement will guide every design, color, bead, wire, component, and finding choice you must make.

Here are 10 color palettes based on emotional statements. I've defined them loosely enough to provide a jump-start, and tightly enough to keep you out of the swampy pit of overwhelmed.

Casual, Happy

Bright, vibrant, saturated jewel tones invite us out to play. Almost any hue works, as long as it's in its pure version (not dulled or lightened) and you use two or more together. Yellows and greens have a summery, citrus flavor. Bright pinks and purples make a playfully feminine scheme (without being too sweet).

Calm, Serene

Pastel versions of cool colors, such as lavender, mint green, and soft sky blue make relaxing, serene palettes. They are gently refreshing and easy on the eyes. These kinds of colors often look good on pale-skinned, light-eyed people.

Earthy, Sensual

Rich, slightly muted warm tones, such as amber, russet, chocolate, and hunter green are the colors of the earth. Add beiges, such as camel and fawn tones. They are sophisticated, alluring, and oh-so-sensual. These often harmonize beautifully on people with honey, deep brown, or coppery hair, and skin that contains olive or yellow undertones.

Passionate, Provocative

Anything—except pastels—in the pink, purple, red, and deep orange range broadcasts passion. They energetically flirt. Add accents of black and gold, and you'll be turning heads left and right.

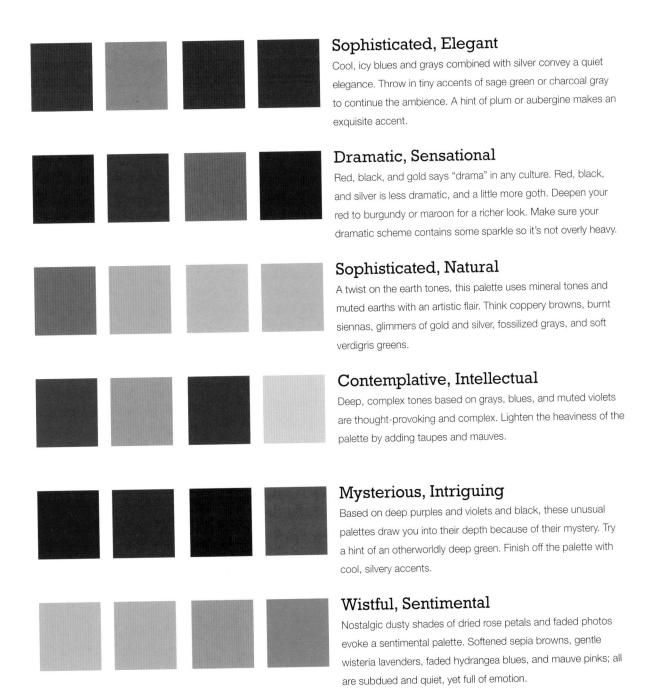

Sophisticated, Elegant

Cool, icy blues and grays combined with silver convey a quiet elegance. Throw in tiny accents of sage green or charcoal gray to continue the ambience. A hint of plum or aubergine makes an exquisite accent.

Dramatic, Sensational

Red, black, and gold says "drama" in any culture. Red, black, and silver is less dramatic, and a little more goth. Deepen your red to burgundy or maroon for a richer look. Make sure your dramatic scheme contains some sparkle so it's not overly heavy.

Sophisticated, Natural

A twist on the earth tones, this palette uses mineral tones and muted earths with an artistic flair. Think coppery browns, burnt siennas, glimmers of gold and silver, fossilized grays, and soft verdigris greens.

Contemplative, Intellectual

Deep, complex tones based on grays, blues, and muted violets are thought-provoking and complex. Lighten the heaviness of the palette by adding taupes and mauves.

Mysterious, Intriguing

Based on deep purples and violets and black, these unusual palettes draw you into their depth because of their mystery. Try a hint of an otherworldly deep green. Finish off the palette with cool, silvery accents.

Wistful, Sentimental

Nostalgic dusty shades of dried rose petals and faded photos evoke a sentimental palette. Softened sepia browns, gentle wisteria lavenders, faded hydrangea blues, and mauve pinks; all are subdued and quiet, yet full of emotion.

Color Your Emotions *was written by Margie Deeb, the author of* The Beader's Color Palette *and* The Beader's Guide to Color. *Margie teaches popular workshops on beading and color throughout the United States. Visit MargieDeeb.com.*

Beading Wire 101

Composition

Most beading wire is composed of multiple strands of steel that are braided together and then coated in nylon. The variations on this basic recipe can include different numbers of strands, varying thickness of nylon, colored nylon, and plating with gold or silver. From manufacturer to manufacturer, there are differences in the quality and origin of the steel and types of nylon, as well as the braid/weave of the wire. Beading wire is typically available as a 7-, 19-, 21-, or 49-strand product. This refers to the number of strands that are braided together to make the wire.

Color

Many beaders shy away from using colored beading wire, even though it should not be intimidating. Using colored beading wire is the perfect way to liven up an average, ordinary design. You now have the option to use the wire as part of the design rather than completely covering it with beads, thereby adding a new dimension of color to the finished piece. Though a strand of colored beading wire will not drastically alter the hue of a transparent bead, it will add to and enhance the bead's color. This results in a richer and more detailed composition.

Diameter

Beading wire is available in four different diameters. Using the correct diameter of wire for the type of bead and style of project is extremely important for ensuring the safety and longevity of your beaded jewelry.

Very Fine—.010 in. diameter wire is best used for sewing, crocheting, knitting, weaving, and embellishing. It's meant to be used like thread.

Fine—.014 in. diameter wire is perfect for basic stringing when using seed beads, pearls, and small stones with holes too small to fit on a thicker diameter wire.

Medium—.019 in. diameter wire is the most commonly used, all-purpose diameter. It's thin enough to fit through most pearls and seed beads and thick enough to handle more abrasive materials such as crystal, glass, and stone.

Heavy—.024 in. diameter wire is best for designs that get a lot of wear and tear, such as bracelets, watch bands, and eyeglass holders. It's strong enough for heavy materials such as lampworked glass, trade beads, and large bone and stone beads.

Beading Wire Comparison

DIAMETER	STRANDS	TEST STRENGTH	BASIC USAGE	CRIMP TUBE TO USE
.014 in. (0.36 mm) Fine	21	10 lbs.	Ideal for soft materials, seed beads, and freshwater pearls.	2 x 2 mm
.019 in. (0.48 mm) Medium	49	26 lbs.	Ideal all-purpose wire. Great with glass, mineral, and metal beads.	2 x 2 mm
.024 in. (0.61 mm) Heavy	49	40 lbs.	Ideal for abrasive materials, large stones, lampwork, and bracelets.	2 x 3 mm

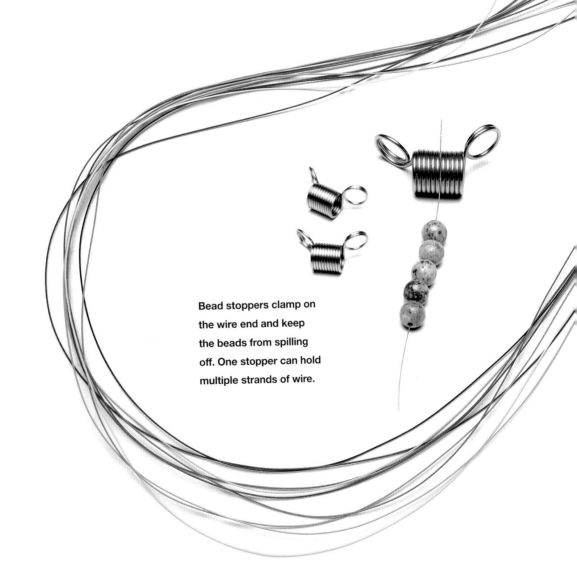

Bead stoppers clamp on the wire end and keep the beads from spilling off. One stopper can hold multiple strands of wire.

Materials 101

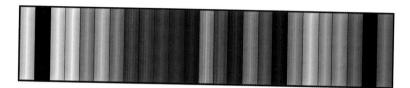

Beading Wire

Clasps

Crimp tubes   Crimp covers   Jump rings

Beading Wire

All projects in this book were made using medium .019 in. diameter wire.

Craft Wire

This gauged wire can be made into findings such as clasps, earring wires, and cones, and is also used for wire-wrapping.

Findings

Clasps are used at the ends of the piece to finish a necklace or bracelet. Clasps are available in many styles, such as toggle, hook-and-eye, magnetic, slide, and box clasps.

Crimp tubes are small tubes of metal used to secure beading wire to clasps and/or connectors. They're available in several sizes, with corresponding crimping pliers used for each size. We used 1 x 1 mm, 2 x 2 mm, and 3 x 3 mm crimp tubes in this book. See Crimping 101 (page 16) for instructions and tips for using crimp tubes.

Crimp covers are small circles of metal used to cover crimp tubes. Once attached, they resemble small round beads.

Jump rings are small circles or ovals of wire used to connect jewelry components. To open and close jump rings, push the ends of the jump ring in opposite directions; do not pull the ends apart or you will ruin the shape of the jump ring.

Earring wires are available in several shapes and sizes and many metals. In addition, craft wire can be used for handmade earring wires specifically suited for a project.

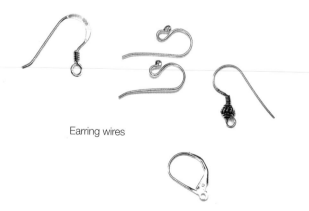

Earring wires

Seed Beads

Available in a variety of sizes, colors, and finishes, seed beads add texture and interest to beaded projects. They are measured in aughts, and the larger the number, the smaller the bead. We've used seed beads ranging in size from 6º to 15º in this book.

Seed Beads

Crystals

We love using a variety of crystal shapes and sizes with our colored flexible beading wire. Bicones, cubes, and rounds are some of the more common shapes.

Crystals

Art Beads

Handmade lampworked beads are full of color and are perfectly paired with colored beading wire.

Art Bead

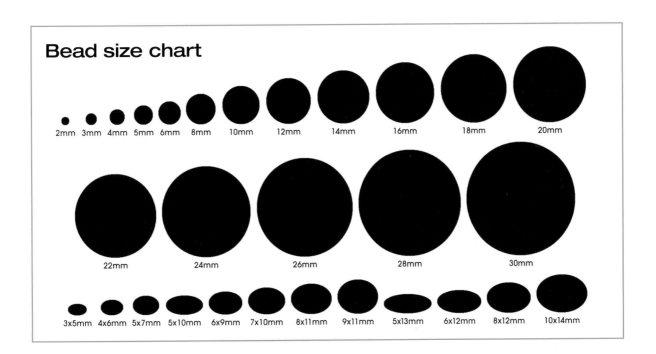

Bead size chart

2mm	3mm	4mm	5mm	6mm	8mm	10mm	12mm	14mm	16mm	18mm	20mm

22mm	24mm	26mm	28mm	30mm

3x5mm	4x6mm	5x7mm	5x10mm	6x9mm	7x10mm	8x11mm	9x11mm	5x13mm	6x12mm	8x12mm	10x14mm

Crimping 101

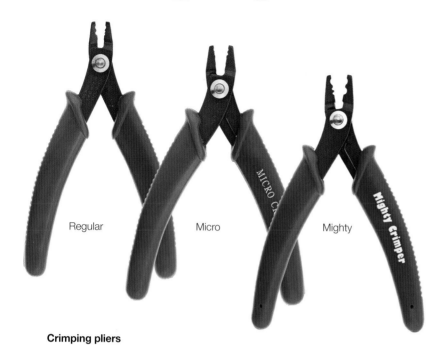

Regular   Micro   Mighty

Crimping pliers

Good-Quality Crimp Tubes

Crimp tubes are so little, it is easy to forget just how important they are. More often than not, crimp tubes hold an entire design together, so it is imperative to use high-quality, seamless crimp tubes. Seamed crimp tubes can easily crack open as you crimp. Therefore, we recommend always using seamless crimp tubes.

How to Crimp

In addition to using seamless crimp tubes, crimping pliers are an equally important part of crimping. Crimping pliers are the safest way to finish a design, as they ensure the crimp tube will securely hold the beading wire in place. We recommend practicing crimping again and again until you're able to make the perfect crimp every time.

Crimping pliers are made up of two holes: a "crimper" and a "rounder" **[a]**. When you reach the end of a bead stringing design, string a crimp tube and one half of your clasp/connector. Pass the wire back through the crimp tube. Snug the crimp tube close to the clasp/connector, making sure to leave enough of a wire loop so that the clasp can easily move around, thereby causing less wear-and-tear on the wire loop **[b]**.

Next, use the "crimper" hole to make a dent in the crimp tube **[c]**. Then, turn the crimp tube 90 degrees and use the "rounder" hole to fold the crimp tube onto

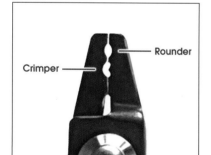

Rounder

Crimper

a

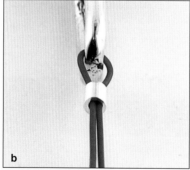

b

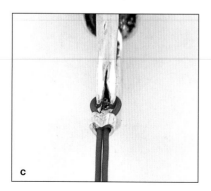

c

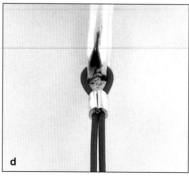

d

itself, securing the wire inside. Use the "rounder" hole to squeeze the crimped tube a few times, slightly rotating the crimped tube each time, to make sure the crimp tube is tight and compact **[d]**.

A properly crimped crimp tube will have no space between the inside of the crimp tube and the wire itself. Make sure not to squeeze the crimping pliers too hard, as you may ruin the structural integrity of the wire and overwork the crimp tube. The pressure necessary to properly secure the crimp tube is the same as what you would use to shake a person's hand. Keep in mind that the purpose of the crimping

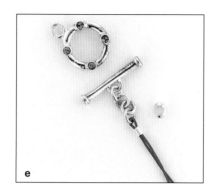

e

pliers is not to smash or crush the crimp tube. Rather, the tool is meant to mold the crimp tube around the wire. Once a crimp tube is correctly crimped to the wire, you have the option of attaching a crimp cover around the tube **[e]**. This can be done with the "rounder" hole of your crimping pliers

f

or with chainnose pliers. Either way works well; it's just a matter of preference. When securing a crimp cover, be sure to rotate the crimp cover a few times while squeezing the pliers so the seam virtually disappears **[f]**.

Choosing the Right Crimp

CRIMP SIZE	BEADING WIRE DIAMETER	How many pieces of wire will fit through the crimp?	CRIMPING PLIERS
1 x 1 mm tube	.014 diameter beading wire	1	Micro Crimping Pliers
2 x 2 mm tube	.014 diameter beading wire	8	Regular Crimping Pliers
3 x 3 mm tube	.014 diameter beading wire	31	Mighty Crimping Pliers
1 x 1 mm tube	.019 diameter beading wire	1	Micro Crimping Pliers
2 x 2 mm tube	.019 diameter beading wire	4	Regular Crimping Pliers
3 x 3 mm tube	.019 diameter beading wire	20	Mighty Crimping Pliers
1 x 1 mm tube	.024 diameter beading wire	0	Micro Crimping Pliers
2 x 2 mm tube	.024 diameter beading wire	1	Regular Crimping Pliers
3 x 3 mm tube	.024 diameter beading wire	10	Mighty Crimping Pliers

Wireworking 101

Wire Cutters

Flush Cutters

Use these to make a flush or diagonal cut in beading wire or craft wire. Do not use these cutters for heavier metals such as memory wire. Place the flat side of these pliers against the wire being cut to get as close and smooth a cut as possible.

Razor Flush Cutters

Use razor flush cutters to make extremely flush cuts in .010 or .014 beading wire only. Do not use these cutters for larger diameters of beading wire or any other type of wire. The tiny points of these cutters make them perfect for getting into small areas such as the very edge of a crimp tube.

Pliers

Roundnose Pliers

These pliers have smooth, tapered, conical jaws and are available in many different diameters and lengths. Roundnose pliers are used to make loops, coils, and, in a pinch, even jump rings. The closer to the tip you work, the smaller the loop will be.

Chainnose Pliers

These pliers have smooth, flat inner jaws and the tips taper to a point. Use them for making sharp bends in wire, for gripping, and for opening and closing loops and jump rings. Though one pair will suffice, it's handy to have two pairs of chainnose pliers in your tool box, especially for projects using several jump rings.

Needlenose Pliers

Similar to chainnose pliers, these have slim, tapered jaws, but are usually much thinner than chainnose. Needlenose pliers are ideal for gripping small items and working in extremely close or tight areas. As with chainnose pliers, always make sure the inside of the jaws are smooth and groove-free.

Wrapped Loop

1 Use roundnose or chainnose pliers to form a 90-degree bend about 1¹/₂ in. (3.8 cm) from one end of the wire **[a]**.

2 Use roundnose pliers to grip the short end of the wire about ¼ in. (6 mm) from the 90-degree bend. Roll the wire toward the bend, making sure to stop just before the bend **[b]**.

3 Use your fingers to bring the wire completely around the roundnose pliers **[c]**.

4 Use chainnose or needlenose pliers to hold the wire loop just formed in your non-dominant hand. Use chainnose or needle-nose pliers to wrap the tail end of the wire two or three times around the wire at the base of the loop, away from the loop **[d]**.

5 Trim the wire end close to the wire at the base of the loop **[e]**. Use chainnose pliers or the "rounder" hole of crimping pliers to help the end of the wire curve around the base wire.

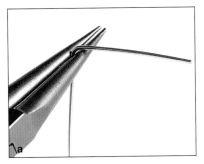

a

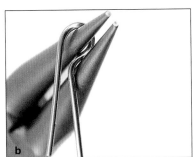

b

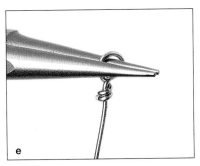

c

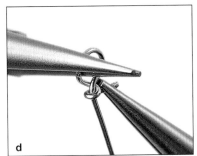

d

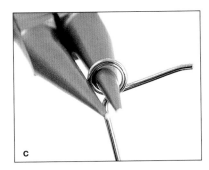

e

Specialty Tools 101

The knitting spool is a simple tool that's been around for ages. It is available with three pegs, four pegs, and five pegs, and every knitting spool comes with a stylus. Wire can be knitted alone, with one strand or several together, and beads can be added to the wire before or during knitting to create a never-ending variety of jewelry designs. The projects in this book were all made with one of two styles of knitting: single wrap and double wrap. All beading wire is knitted directly from the wire spool to the knitting spool.

Style 1: Single Wrap

Pass the wire end(s) down through the center of the knitting spool, from top to bottom. Adjust the wire(s) so that there are a couple of inches sticking out below the spool. Hold the wire end(s) securely in your non-dominant hand.

Wrap the wire clockwise completely around one peg of the knitting spool. Move the wire counter-clockwise to the next peg **[a]**. Repeat around all pegs **[b]**.

After all pegs are wrapped, bring the wire around the outside of the first peg wrapped. Turn the spool so that the first peg is facing you **[c]**. Use the stylus to bring the initial wrapped wire loop up and over the peg. Keep the stylus pressed up against the peg as much as possible as you do this, to help ensure an even tension throughout the project.

Gently pull down on the wire ends after each knitted stitch. Repeat around the spool until the design is the desired length. Cut the wire(s) off the wire spool, leaving a 10-in. (25 cm) tail. Working around the spool, pass the wire end(s) through every wire loop on the knitting spool. Once the wire end(s) has passed through a wire loop, carefully remove the wire loop from the knitting spool. Pull the knitted cord out of the knitting spool. Pull tightly on the end(s) of the knitted cord, tightening the last few stitches as much as possible.

Style 2: Double Wrap

Pass the wire end(s) down through the center of the knitting spool, from top to bottom. Adjust the wire(s) so that there are a couple of inches sticking out below the spool. Hold the wire end(s) securely in your non-dominant hand.

Wrap the wire clockwise completely around one peg of the knitting spool. Move the wire counter-clockwise to the next peg.

Repeat around all pegs.

Repeat to wrap completely around the first peg wrapped again, so that there are two wire wraps around the peg **[d]**.

Turn the spool so that the first peg is facing you. Use the stylus to bring the initial wrapped wire loop up and over the second wrapped wire loop **[e]**. Keep the stylus pressed up against the peg as much as possible as you do this, to help ensure an even tension throughout the project.

Repeat around the spool until the design is the desired length. Cut the wire(s) off the wire spool, leaving a 10-in. (25 cm) tail. Working around the spool, pass the wire end(s) through every wire loop on the knitting spool. Once the wire end(s) has passed through a wire loop, carefully remove the wire loop from the knitting spool. Pull the knitted cord out of the knitting spool. Pull tightly on the end(s) of the knitted cord, tightening the last few stitches as much as possible.

Knitting Spools

Specialty Tools 101

Nylon Hammer

Bench Block

WigJig®

Nylon Hammer

This hammer is used to shape or work harden wire without leaving marks.

Bench Block

Made of hardened steel, use it to hammer and form metal.

WigJig®

This handy tool makes uniform wire shapes. Pegs come in a variety of diameters; set them in a pattern and simply coil craft wire around them to create a shape.

Speeder Beader

This oversized "needle" grips the beading wire and makes it easier to string larger, hollow beads.

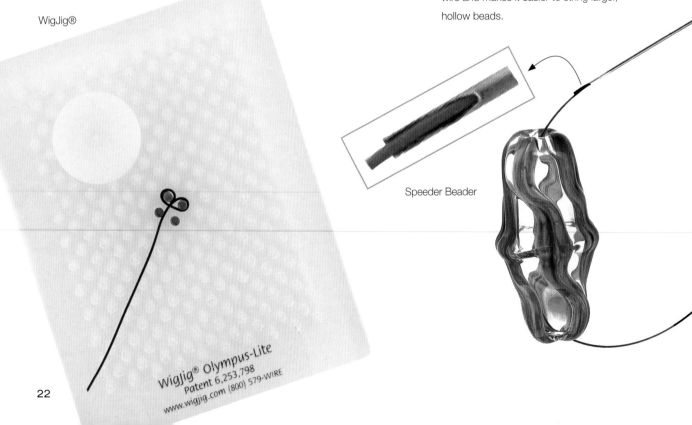

Speeder Beader

WigJig® Olympus-Lite
Patent 6,253,798
www.wigjig.com (800) 579-WIRE

Chapter 1

NOT SO
SIMPLY
STRUNG

Show your colors by using colored beading wire as a
component in your strung designs. In fact, use the wire
to enhance and complement beads and create snazzy,
successful pieces. All the projects in this chapter bring
a creative flair to stringing beads on a wire. Create links
and dangles, and learn how to suspend a bead in place
on wire by crimping or looping. And don't forget, your
choice of color can make a large impact.

Mirror Image

Colored beading wire and seed beads blend together to provide the only pop of color in these black, metal-based earrings. Red and white wires woven through spacers and red and lavender seed beads create a whimsical pair of dangles. To further the color play, using red wire with pale lavender beads and white wire with red beads makes two strands look entirely different, even though the pattern is similar.

materials

- Beading Wire (.019):
  16 in. (41 cm) white quartz
  16 in. red coral
  16 in. black onyx
- **4** 10 mm gunmetal large-hole large coiled rings
- **10** 6 mm gunmetal large-hole small coiled rings
- **6** 8 mm gunmetal large-hole beaded daisy spacers
- **6** 6 mm gunmetal beaded daisy spacers
- **44** 11º crystal matte seed beads
- **44** 11º red matte seed beads
- **4** 4 mm milky light amethyst Czech pressed-glass rondelles
- **4** 4 mm Siam ruby Czech pressed-glass rondelles
- **30** 2 x 2 mm gunmetal crimp tubes
- pair of gunmetal earring wires

tools

- crimping pliers
- wire cutters

*Finished Size:
3½ in. (8.9 cm)*

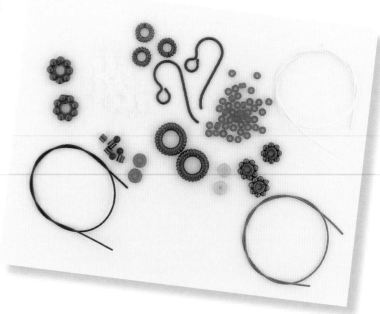

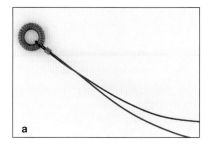

a

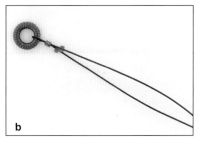

b

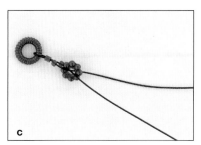

c

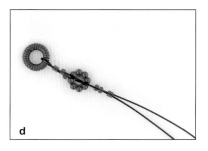

d

1 Center a 10 mm coiled ring on 8 in. (20 cm) of black onyx beading wire. String a crimp tube over both ends. Snug the crimp tube up to the ring, and crimp **[a]**.

2 String a red 11º seed bead on each wire **[b]**.

3 String an 8 mm daisy spacer on one wire. Come back through the spacer in the opposite direction with the other wire **[c]**.

4 String a red 11º on each wire, and then string a crimp tube over both wires. Position the crimp ½ in. (1.3 cm) away from the crimp from Step 1, and crimp **[d]**.

5 Repeat Step 2 using crystal 11º seed beads. Repeat Step 3 using a 6 mm coiled ring. Repeat Step 4 using crystal 11ºs.

6 Repeat Step 2. Repeat Step 3 using a 6 mm daisy spacer. Repeat Step 4.

7 Repeat Step 2 using crystal 11ºs. Repeat Step 3 using a 10 mm large coiled ring. Repeat Step 4 using crystal 11ºs and placing the crimp about ⅝ in. (1.6 cm) from the previous crimp. Trim the wire ends.

8 Center the 10 mm large coiled ring from Step 1 on 8 in. of red coral beading wire. String a crimp tube over both wires. Snug the crimp tube to the ring, and crimp. Repeat Step 5.

9 On one end of the wire, string a crystal 11º. On the other end of the wire, string a milky light amethyst rondelle. On one end of the wire, string a 6 mm daisy spacer. On the other end of the wire, go back through the spacer in the opposite direction. On one end of the wire, string a crystal 11º. On the other end of the wire, string a crystal 11º. String a crimp tube over both wires. Adjust the crimp tube so that it is about ½ in. from the previous crimp tube, and crimp.

10 Repeat Step 5. Repeat Step 9 using an 8 mm daisy spacer. Trim the wire ends.

11 Center the 10 mm large coiled ring from Step 1 on 8 in. of white quartz beading wire. String a crimp tube over both wires. Snug the crimp tube to the ring, and crimp.

12 Repeat Step 2. On one end of the wire, string a 6 mm coiled ring. Go back through the coiled ring with the other wire in the opposite direction. On one end of the wire, string a red 11º. On the other end of the wire, string a Siam ruby rondelle. String a crimp tube over both wires. Adjust the crimp tube so that it is about ½ in. from the previous crimp tube, and crimp.

13 Repeat Step 6. Repeat Step 12. Repeat Step 6 using an 8 mm daisy spacer. Trim the wire ends.

14 Attach an earring wire to the 10 mm coiled ring from Step 1.

15 Make a second earring, making sure when attaching the earring wire that the earrings are mirror images of each other.

Dark Lady

This necklace is light and delicate despite the multi-strand design and large crystal focal beads. Colored beading wire not only adds to the length and airiness of the project, it serves as a method of anchoring the focal beads. It also gives dimension to the piece, with each wire color complementing one of the crystal colors.

materials

- Beading Wire (.019):
  30 in. (76 cm) tanzanite
  32 in. (81 cm) bone
  34 in. (86 cm) garnet
  1 yd. (.9 m) imperial topaz
- **13** 11 x 12 mm crystal copper crystal cosmic beads
- **4** 6 x 9 mm light Colorado topaz crystal teardrops
- **5** 8 mm light Colorado topaz crystal rounds
- **2** 6 mm light Colorado topaz crystal rounds
- **20** 6 mm maroon crystal pearls
- **10** 6 mm night blue crystal pearls
- **12** 4 mm light Colorado topaz crystal rounds
- **4** gold-filled 2 x 2 mm crimp tubes
- **4** 2 x 2 mm gold-filled crimp covers
- **15 x 20 mm** antique gold pewter heirloom toggle clasp

tools

- crimping pliers
- wire cutters
- bead stoppers

Finished Size: 20¼ in. (51.4 cm)

a

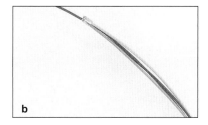

b

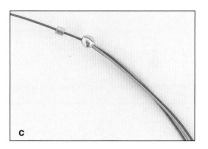

c

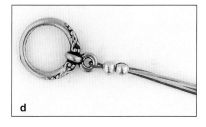

d

1 Place a bead stopper on an end of the garnet wire. Center a blue pearl, an 8 mm round, and a blue pearl on the wire.

2 String a cosmic bead. Pass the wire through the bead again, creating a wire loop around the bead **[a]**.

3 String a blue pearl, an 8 mm round, and a blue pearl. Repeat Step 2 1½ in. (3.8 cm) from the previous cosmic bead.

4 Remove the bead stopper and repeat Steps 2 and 3 on the other end. Set aside.

5 Repeat Step 2 to center a cosmic bead on the butterscotch wire. On one end, string a maroon pearl, an 8 mm round, and a maroon pearl. Repeat Step 2 1½ in. from the previous cosmic bead. String a blue pearl, a teardrop, and a blue pearl. Place a bead stopper on one wire end. On the other end, string a blue pearl, an 8 mm round, and a blue pearl. Repeat Step 2. String a maroon pearl, a teardrop, and a maroon pearl. Place a bead stopper on the wire end. Set aside.

6 Repeat Step 2 to center a cosmic bead on the bone wire. *String a 4 mm round, a maroon pearl, a teardrop, a maroon pearl, and a 4 mm round. Repeat Step 2 2 in. (5 cm) from the previous cosmic bead. String a 4 mm round, a maroon pearl, a 6 mm round, a maroon pearl, and a 4 mm round. Place a bead stopper on the wire. Repeat from * on the other end. Set aside.

7 Repeat Step 2 to center a cosmic bead on the tanzanite wire. *String a maroon pearl, a 4 mm round, and a maroon pearl. Repeat Step 2 1 in. (2.5 cm) from the previous cosmic bead. String a maroon pearl, a 4 mm round, and a maroon pearl. Place a bead stopper on the wire end. Repeat from * on the other end of the wire.

8 Remove bead stoppers from one end of each wire. String a crimp tube over all four wires. Place a bead stopper on the wire ends.

9 Repeat Step 8 on the other wire ends. Adjust wire and crimp tubes so that all strung beads are centered on each strand and (between crimp tubes) the tanzanite strand is 23 in. (58 cm), the bone strand is 25 in. (64 cm), the garnet strand is 27 in. (69 cm), and the butterscotch strand is 29 in. (74 cm). Crimp the crimp tubes.

10 On one end, cut all wires except the garnet **[b]**.

11 Cover the crimp tube with a crimp cover. String a crimp tube and half the clasp on the garnet wire **[c]**. Go back through the tube and crimp. Cover the crimp tube with a crimp cover **[d]**.

12 Repeat Steps 10 and 11 on the other end.

27

Rain Rain

Four subtly different colors of beading wire in shades of green and blue look like little raindrops when wrapped around seed beads in this 12-strand bracelet. The small wire circles add textural interest to this otherwise simply strung cuff. Coordinating strands of seed beads provide a great contrast in texture to the airy wire strands.

materials

- Beading Wire (.019):
  25 in. (64 cm) turquoise
  25 in. peridot
  25 in. fluorite
  25 in. chrysoprase
- **157** 11º shimmering seafoam-lined seed beads
- **157** 11º citrine/lime-lined seed beads

- **157** 11º wintergreen opal gilt-lined seed beads
- **157** 11º metallic light peridot-lined transparent citrine seed beads
- **15** 8º opaque matte turquoise seed beads
- **15** 8º silver lined transparent opal mint green seed beads
- **30** 8º light blue-lined transparent lightest amber seed beads

- **6** 6º aqua light bronze rococo silver-lined seed beads
- **14** 2 x 2 mm sterling silver crimp tubes
- **14** 3 mm sterling silver crimp covers
- 52 x 34 mm Thai silver 7-strand hook-and-eye clasp

tools

- crimping pliers
- wire cutters

Finished Size: 6 in. (15 cm)

For a longer bracelet, cut three additional inches of wire for each additional inch of length and extend the beaded pattern.

1 Pair the 25-in. (64 cm) lengths of turquoise and peridot beading wires. String a crimp tube, a 6º seed bead, and the fourth/middle loop of the hook half of the clasp. Pass both wire ends back through the seed bead and the crimp tube, and crimp **[a]**. Cover the crimp tube with a crimp cover **[b]**.

2 On the peridot beading wire, string a silver-lined transparent opal mint green 8º seed bead. Place the seed bead about ½ in. (1.3 cm) from the previous bead. Pass the wire through the seed bead again, forming a loop of wire around the seed bead **[c]**. Repeat six times.

3 String a crimp tube and the fifth loop of the eye half of the clasp. Pass back through the tube, adjust the wire so that there is about 5½ in. (14 cm) of wire between this crimp tube and the previous crimp tube, and crimp. Do not trim the wire end. Cover the crimp tube with a crimp cover.

4 Continue working with the peridot wire. String 85 citrine/lime-lined 11º seed beads, a crimp tube, a 6º seed bead, and the sixth loop of the hook half of the clasp. Pass back through the seed bead and the crimp tube, adjust the wire so that there are about 5½ in. of wire between this crimp tube and the previous crimp tube, and crimp. Cover the crimp tube with a crimp cover. Do not trim the wire.

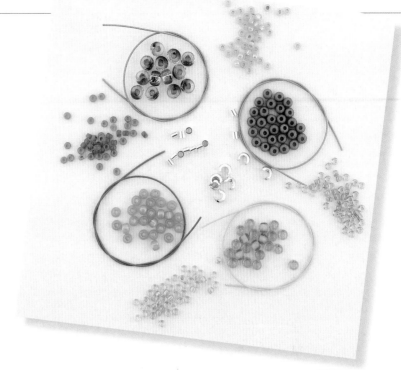

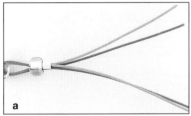
a

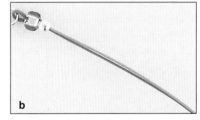
b

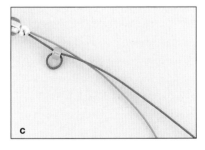
c

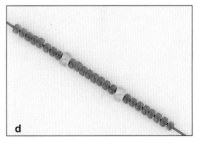
d

5 Continue working with the peridot wire. String {eight citrine/lime-lined 11º seed beads and a silver-lined transparent opal mint green 8º seed bead} eight times **[d]**. String eight 11ºs, a crimp tube, and the seventh loop of the eye half of the clasp. Pass back through the crimp tube, adjust the wire so that there is about 5½ in. of wire between the crimp tubes and crimp. Trim excess wire. Cover the crimp with a crimp cover.

6 Pick up the turquoise beading wire from Step 1 and string 85 shimmering seafoam-lined 11º seed beads. String a crimp tube and the third loop of the eye half of the clasp. Pass back through the crimp tube, adjust the wire so that there is about 5½ in. of wire between the crimp tubes, and crimp. Cover the crimp tube with a crimp cover. Do not trim the wire.

7 Continue working with the turquoise wire. String an opaque matte turquoise 8° seed bead about ½ in. from the previous bead. Pass the wire through the 8° again, forming a loop of wire around the seed bead. Repeat six times.

8 String a crimp tube, a 6° seed bead, and the second loop of the hook half of the clasp. Pass back through the 6° and the crimp, adjust the wire so there is about 5½ in. of wire between the crimp tubes, and crimp. Cover the crimps with a crimp cover.

9 Continue working with the turquoise wire. String {eight shimmering seafoam-lined 11° seed beads and a opaque matte turquoise 8° seed bead} eight times. String eight seafoam 11°s, a crimp tube, and the first loop of the eye half of the clasp. Pass back through the crimp, adjust the wire so there is about 5½ in. of wire between the crimp tubes, and crimp. Trim excess wire. Cover the crimp with a crimp cover.

10 Pair 25 in. of fluorite (shown in black on the diagram) wire and 25 in. of chrysoprase (shown in red) wire. String a crimp tube, a 6° seed bead, and the fourth/middle loop of the eye half of the clasp. Pass both ends back through the 6° and the crimp tube, and crimp. Cover with a crimp cover.

11 With the chrysoprase wire, string a light blue-lined transparent lightest amber 8° seed bead. Place the 8° about ½ in. from the previous bead. Pass the wire through the seed bead again, forming a loop of wire around the seed bead. Repeat six times.

12 String a crimp tube and the third loop of the hook half of the clasp. Pass back through the crimp, adjust the wire so that there is about 5½ in. of wire between the crimp tubes, and crimp. Cover the crimp with a crimp cover. Do not trim the wire.

13 Continue working with the chrysoprase wire. String 85 metallic light peridot-lined transparent citrine 11° seed beads, a crimp tube, a 6°, and the second loop of the eye half of the clasp. Pass back through the seed bead and the crimp tube, adjust the wire so that there is about 5½ in. of wire between the crimp tubes, and crimp. Cover the crimp with a crimp cover. Do not trim.

14 Continue working with the chrysoprase beading wire. String {eight metallic light peridot-lined transparent citrine 11° seed beads and a light blue-lined transparent lightest amber 8° seed bead} eight times. String eight metallic light peridot-lined transparent citrine 11° seed beads, a crimp tube, and the first loop of the hook half of the clasp. Pass back through the crimp

tube, adjust the wire so there is about 5½ in. of wire between the crimp tubes, and crimp. Trim excess wire. Cover the crimp with a crimp cover.

15 Pick up the fluorite wire from Step 10. String 85 wintergreen opal gilt-lined 11° seed beads. String a crimp tube and the fifth loop of the hook half of the clasp. Pass back through the seed bead and the crimp tube, adjust the wire so that there is about 5½ in. of wire between the crimp tubes, and crimp. Cover the crimp tube with a crimp cover. Do not trim.

16 Continue working with the fluorite wire. String a light blue lined transparent lightest amber 8° seed bead. Place the seed bead about ½ in. from the previous bead. Pass the wire through the seed bead again, forming a loop of wire around the seed bead. Repeat six times.

17 String a crimp tube, a 6°, and the sixth loop of the eye half of the clasp. Pass back through the seed bead and the crimp tube, adjust the wire so that there is about 5½ in. of wire between the crimp tubes, and crimp. Cover the crimp tube with a crimp cover. Do not trim.

18 Continue working with the fluorite wire. String {eight wintergreen opal gilt-lined 11° seed beads and a light blue lined transparent lightest amber 8° seed bead} eight times. String eight wintergreen opal gilt-lined seed beads, a crimp tube, and the seventh loop of the hook half of the clasp. Pass back through the crimp tube, adjust the wire so that there is about 5½ in. of wire between the crimp tubes, and crimp. Trim excess wire. Cover the crimp tube with a crimp cover.

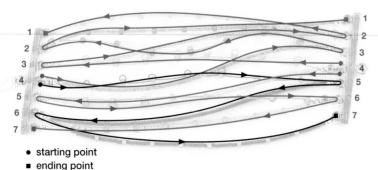

• starting point
■ ending point

Melody

In these earrings the colored beading wire plays a supporting role. This harmonious design plays all the right notes for a perfect melody. A subtle color can go a long way but still make a large impact.

1 On 2 in. (5 cm) of beading wire, string a crimp tube and an earring wire. Go back through the tube, leaving a small open loop and crimp. String an 11º seed bead, a 4 mm crystal, an 11º, and a crimp tube. Go back through the tube and crimp **[a]**.

2 On 2 in. of wire, string a crimp tube and the open loop created in Step 1. Go back through the tube, leaving a small open loop and crimp. String an 11º, a 6 mm crystal, an 11º, and a crimp tube. Go back through the tube and crimp **[b]**.

3 On 2 in. of wire, string a crimp tube and the open loop created in Step 2. Go back through the tube and crimp. String an 11º, an 8 mm crystal, an 11º, and a crimp tube. Snug the beads and crimp the crimp tube. Trim the wire just under the crimp **[c]**.

4 Make a second earring.

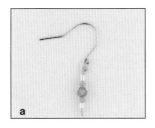
a

b

c

materials

- Beading Wire (.019): 12 in. (30 cm) chrysoprase
- **2** 8 mm peridot crystal bicones
- **2** 6 mm peridot crystal bicones
- **2** 4 mm peridot crystal bicones
- **12** 11º opaque yellow seed beads
- **12** 2 x 2 mm sterling silver crimp tubes
- Pair of sterling silver earring wires

tools

- crimping pliers
- wire cutters

Finished Size: 2¼ in. (5.7 cm)

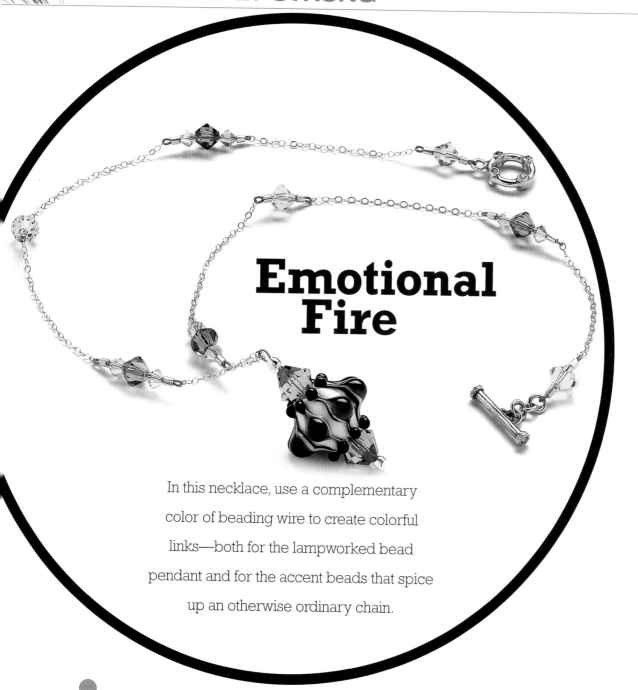

Emotional Fire

In this necklace, use a complementary color of beading wire to create colorful links—both for the lampworked bead pendant and for the accent beads that spice up an otherwise ordinary chain.

materials

- Beading Wire (.019): 18 in. (46 cm) citrine
- 21 x 14 mm topaz/black/cream lampworked crown bead (Nancy Pilgrim)
- **2** 8 mm topaz crystal bicones
- **4** 6 mm citrine crystal bicones
- **4** 6 mm topaz crystal bicones
- **8** 4 mm citrine crystal bicones
- **18** 2 x 2 mm sterling silver crimp tubes
- **2** 3 mm sterling silver crimp covers
- 11 in. (28 cm) sterling silver chain
- 12 mm sterling silver toggle clasp with topaz crystal inlay

tools

- crimping pliers
- wire cutters

Finished Size: 17¾ in. (45.1 cm)

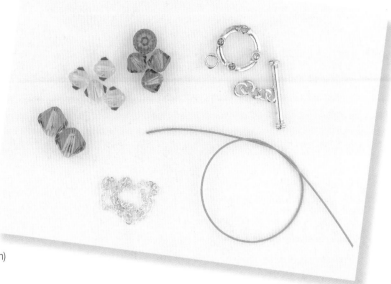

1 Cut the chain into seven 1½ in. (3.8 cm) pieces. Set aside.

2 On 2 in. (5 cm) of beading wire, string a crimp tube. Go back through the tube, creating a loop that is big enough to slide over the chain, and crimp. Cover the tube with a crimp cover. String an 8 mm topaz crystal, the lampworked crown bead, an 8 mm topaz crystal, and a crimp tube. Snug the beads and crimp the crimp tube next to the crystal. Cover the tube with a crimp cover. Set aside **[a, b]**.

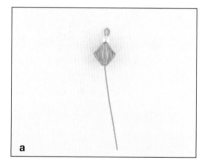

a

b

3 On 2 in. of beading wire, string a crimp tube and one half of the clasp. Go back through the tube and crimp. String a 6 mm citrine crystal, a crimp tube, and one end of a chain piece. Go back through the tube and crimp **[c]**.

c

4 On 2 in. of beading wire, string a crimp tube and the other end of the chain piece from the previous step. Go back through the tube and crimp. String a 4 mm citrine crystal, a 6 mm topaz crystal, a 4 mm citrine crystal, a crimp tube, and one end of a chain piece. Go back through the tube and crimp.

5 On 2 in. of beading wire, string a crimp tube and the other end of the chain from the previous step. Go back through the tube and crimp. String a 6 mm citrine crystal, a crimp tube, and one end of a chain piece. Go back through the tube and crimp.

6 Repeat Step 4.

7 On the the end of the chain, string the dangle created in Step 1 **[d]**.

8 Repeat Step 4.

d

9 Repeat Step 5.

10 Repeat Step 4.

11 On 2 in. of beading wire, string a crimp tube and the other end of the chain. Go back through the tube and crimp. String a 6 mm citrine crystal, a crimp tube, and the other half of the clasp. Go back through the tube and crimp.

Angels Running

Use a contrasting color of beading wire to create consistent crystal links.

A little pop of color can go a long way.

materials

- Beading Wire (.019): 16 in. (41 cm) turquoise
- **8** 8 mm light Colorado topaz crystal bicones
- **16** 11º matte opaque turquoise seed beads
- **9** 5 mm sterling silver jump rings
- **16** 2 x 2 mm sterling silver crimp tubes
- **16** 3 mm sterling silver crimp covers
- 8 mm sterling silver star box clasp

tools

- chainnose pliers
- crimping pliers
- wire cutters

Finished Size: 8 in. (20 cm)

a

b

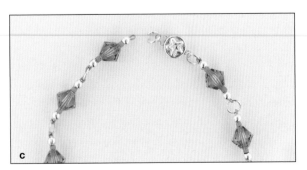

c

Make the jump ring connections as secure as you can to prevent the beading wire from slipping through. Alternately, use soldered jump rings for all the connections except to attach the clasp.

1 Attach a jump ring to a clasp half. On 2 in. (5 cm) of beading wire, string a crimp tube and a jump ring. Go back through the tube and crimp. Cover the tube with a crimp cover. String an 11º seed bead, an 8 mm crystal, an 11º, a crimp, and the jump ring. Go back through the crimp tube and crimp. Cover the crimp with a crimp cover **[a]**.

2 On 2 in. of beading wire, string a crimp tube and the previous jump ring. Go back through the tube and crimp; cover with a crimp cover. String an 11º, an 8 mm crystal, an 11º, a crimp, and a jump ring. Go back through the tube and crimp; cover with a crimp cover **[b]**.

3 Repeat Step 2 six times, or until the bracelet is desired length. Attach the final jump ring to the other half of the clasp **[c]**.

Chapter 2

BEYOND ILLUSION

Illusion-style jewelry is the perfect way to incorporate colored beading wire into your designs. Blending bead colors with wire colors makes these delicate designs dance.

Magic in the Air

This multi-strand necklace uses floral silver beads in different shapes to unite five colors of beading wire. Using wire colors similar to those found in a flower bed, means the one little ladybug bead in the necklace looks like she's leisurely living in a beautiful garden.

materials

- Beading Wire (.019):
  24 in. (61 cm) peridot
  24 in. chrysoprase
  24 in. purple amethyst
  24 in. spinel
  24 in. pink rhodochrosite
- 8 x 10 mm antique silver pewter ladybug bead
- **10** 7 mm antique silver pewter floral rounds
- **10** 6 x 10 mm antique silver pewter wild rose ovals
- **10** 6 x 10 mm antique silver pewter trillium ovals
- **27** 6 x 3 mm antique silver pewter four flowers spacers
- **82** 2 x 2 mm (small) sterling silver crimp tubes
- **2** 3 x 3 mm (large) sterling silver crimp tubes
- **82** 3 mm sterling silver crimp covers
- **2** 4 mm sterling silver crimp covers
- 7 x 23 mm antique silver pewter vine hook-and-eye clasp

tools

- crimping pliers
- mighty crimping pliers
- wire cutters
- bead stoppers

Finished Size: 21 in. (53 cm)

1 Place a bead stopper on one end of the peridot beading wire. String a 2 x 2 mm (small) crimp tube, a wild rose oval, two small crimps, three flower spacers, two small crimps, a floral round, two small crimps, a trillium oval, two small crimps, a wild rose oval, two small crimps, the ladybug bead (bottom to top), two small crimps, a floral round, two small crimps, a trillium oval, and a small crimp. Place a bead stopper on the other end of the wire. Set aside.

2 Place a bead stopper on one end of the chrysoprase beading wire. String a small crimp tube. String a trillium oval, two small crimps, a floral round, two small crimps, three flower spacers, two small crimps, a wild rose oval, and two small crimps. Repeat the pattern, omitting the final crimp tube. Place a bead stopper on the other end of the wire. Set aside.

3 Place a bead stopper on one end of the purple amethyst beading wire. String a small crimp tube. String three flower spacers, two small crimps, a wild rose oval, two small crimps, a trillium oval, two small crimps, a floral round, and two small crimps. Repeat the pattern, omitting the final crimp tube. Place a bead stopper on the other end of the wire. Set aside.

4 Place a bead stopper on one end of the spinel beading wire. String one small crimp tube. String a floral round, two small crimps, a trillium oval, two small crimps, a wild rose oval, two small crimps, three flower spacers, and two small crimps. Repeat the pattern, omitting

the final crimp tube. Place a bead stopper on the other end of the wire. Set aside.

5 Place a bead stopper on one end of the pink rhodochrosite beading wire. String a small crimp tube. String a trillium oval, two small crimps, a wild rose oval, two small crimps, three flower spacers, two small crimps, a floral round, and two small crimps. Repeat the pattern, omitting the final crimp tube. Place a bead stopper on the other end of the wire. Set aside.

6 Remove a bead stopper from one end of each wire. Over all five wires, string a large 3 x 3 mm crimp tube. Place it 2 in. (5 cm) from the wire ends **[a]** and crimp using mighty crimping pliers. Cover with a 4 mm crimp cover.

a

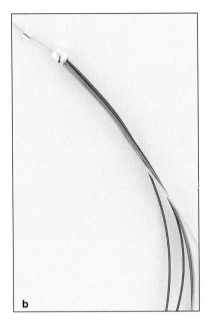

b

c

7 Cut the wire ends of all but the chrysoprase beading wire. Use the chrysoprase beading wire to string a small crimp tube **[b]** and one half of the clasp. Go back through the tube and crimp. Cover the crimp tube with a 3 mm crimp cover.

8 Repeat Steps 6 and 7 for the other end of the necklace **[c]**.

9 Place the first crimp tube strung on the peridot beading wire about ½ in. (1.3 cm) from the 4 mm crimp cover, and crimp. Cover the crimp tube with a 3 mm crimp cover. Snug the pewter bead and the crimp tube, and crimp the tube. Cover with a 3 mm crimp cover.

10 Place the next crimp tube strung 1½ –2 in. (3.8–5 cm) from the previous crimp cover, and crimp. Cover the crimp tube with a 3 mm crimp cover. Snug the pewter bead and the crimp tube, and crimp the tube. Cover with a 3 mm crimp cover. Repeat six times.

11 Place the first crimp tube strung on the chrysoprase beading wire about 1 in. (2.5 cm) from the 4 mm crimp cover, and crimp. Cover the crimp tube with a 3 mm crimp cover. Snug the pewter bead and the crimp tube, and crimp the tube. Cover with a 3 mm crimp cover. Repeat Step 10.

12 Place the first crimp tube strung on the purple amethyst beading wire about 1¾ in. (4.4 cm) from the 4 mm crimp cover, and crimp. Cover the crimp tube with a 3 mm crimp cover. Snug the pewter bead and the crimp tube, and crimp the tube. Cover with a 3 mm crimp cover. Repeat Step 10.

13 Place the first crimp tube strung on the spinel beading wire about 3 in. from the 4 mm crimp cover, and crimp. Cover the crimp tube with a 3 mm crimp cover. Snug the pewter bead and the crimp tube, and crimp the tube. Cover with a 3 mm crimp cover. Repeat Step 10.

14 Place the first crimp tube strung on the pink rhodochrosite beading wire about 1¾ in. from the 4 mm crimp cover, and crimp. Cover the crimp tube with a 3 mm crimp cover. Snug the pewter bead and the crimp tube, and crimp the tube. Cover with a 3 mm crimp cover. Repeat Step 10.

How Pretty the Moon

Three dark wire colors exposed between dark purple beads and gold findings blend to create a dramatic pair of hoop earrings. Using beads of the same color and varying the wire colors lets the wire give the most interest to the design. The colored wire and the effervescent beads keep the eyes moving around the pair—eye-catching indeed.

materials
- Beading Wire (.019):
  22 in. (56 cm) purple amethyst
  22 in. blue topaz
  22 in. green emerald
- **10** 6 mm dark purple crystal pearls
- **18** 4 mm tanzanite fire-polished rounds
- **2** 6 x 16 mm antique gold pewter heishi large 3-hole spacer bars
- **4** 6 x 12 mm antique gold pewter heishi small 3-hole spacer bars
- **28** 2 x 2 mm gold-filled crimp tubes
- **48** 1 x 1 mm gold-filled crimp tubes
- **28** 3 mm gold-filled crimp covers
- pair of gold-filled earring wires

tools
- crimping pliers
- micro crimping pliers
- wire cutters

Finished Size: 3¾ in. (7.6 cm)

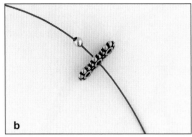

a

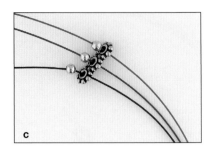

b

c

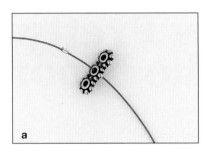

d

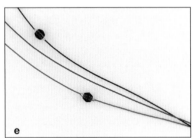

e

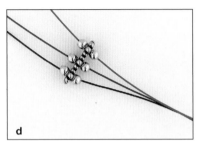

f

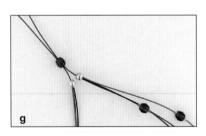

g

h

1 Cut each color of beading wire into two 11-in. (28 cm) lengths.

2 Center the middle hole of the large 3-hole spacer on an 11-in. length of purple wire. String a 2 x 2 mm crimp tube on one end. Crimp **[a]** and cover with a crimp cover **[b]**.

3 Repeat Step 2 with 11-in. lengths of green and blue wire through the remaining holes in the spacer **[c]**.

4 On the other end of each wire, string a 2 x 2 mm crimp tube and snug to the bar link. Crimp and cover with a crimp cover **[d]**.

5 On one end of the blue wire, string a 1 x 1 mm crimp tube, a 4 mm round, and a 1 x 1 mm crimp. Place the first crimp strung about ⅛ in. (3 mm) from the previous crimp cover and crimp using micro crimping pliers. Snug the beads and crimp the second crimp strung. Repeat using the green wire and place the first crimp string about ¾ in. (1.9 cm) from the previous crimp cover **[e]**.

6 On the purple wire, string a 1 x 1 mm crimp tube, a pearl, and a 1 x 1 mm crimp. Place the first crimp strung about ⅜ in. (1 cm) from the previous crimp cover and crimp. Snug the beads and crimp the second crimp strung.

7 On the purple wire , string a 2 x 2 mm crimp tube. Place the crimp ⅜ in. from the previous crimp. Crimp and cover with a crimp cover. String the center hole of a small 3-hole heishi and a 2 x 2 mm crimp tube. Snug the beads. Crimp and cover with a crimp cover. On the blue wire, string the right hole of the link. On the green wire, string the left hole of the link.

8 Repeat Steps 5 and 6, measuring from the heishi strung in Step 7. On all three wires together, string a 2 x 2 mm crimp tube. Place the crimp about 1 in. from the previous crimp on the blue wire, about ½ in. (1.3 cm) from the previous crimp on the purple wire, and about ¼ in. (6 mm) from the previous crimp on the green wire. Crimp. Trim the ends of the blue and green wires. Do not cut the purple wire. Cover the tube with a crimp cover **[f]**.

9 Repeat Steps 5–8 for the other half of the earring, alternating the bead placement on the blue and green wires.

10 On both ends of the purple wires, string a 4 mm round **[g]**. On both ends, string a 2 x 2 mm crimp tube. Snug the beads and crimp. Trim one end. Cover the crimp tube with a crimp cover **[h]**.

11 String a pearl, a 2 x 2 mm crimp tube, and an earring wire. Go back through the crimp. Crimp and cover with a crimp cover.

12 Make a second earring.

Holy Smoke

This wide cuff pairs seed beads with colored beading wire to form long links with lots of movement. Crimp tubes keep the seed beads spaced on the links, and since they don't fill the length, it's a sure bet that there will always be a small bit of colored wire showing.

materials

- Beading Wire (.019):
  91½ in. (2.325 m) bronze
  52 in. (1.32 m) peridot
  52 in. black onyx
- **12** 7 mm antique silver casbah rounds
- **10** 8 mm antique brass crystal pearls
- **4** 6 mm antique brass crystal pearls
- **129** 11º dark brown matte metallic seed beads
- **112** 11º bronze metallic cut seed beads
- **127** 11º chartreuse matte seed beads
- **117** 11º black opaque seed beads
- **96** 2 x 2 mm sterling silver crimp tubes
- **96** 3 mm sterling silver crimp covers
- **2** 10 x 20 mm sterling silver magnetic clasps

tools

- crimping pliers
- wire cutters

Finished Size:
7¼ in. (18.4 cm)

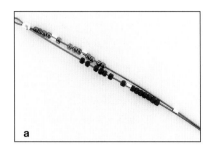

a

b

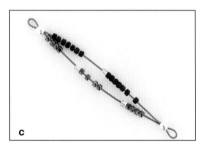

c

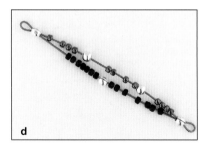

d

Make 20 horizontal components

You will make single and double-strand components. Later, you will string them in the order you've made them, so keep your workspace organized.

For a single-strand component, use 6 in. (15 cm) of wire. String a crimp tube on one end. Go back through the crimp, leaving a small loop, and crimp. String beads and crimp tubes in the pattern described below, and finish with a crimp tube. Place the final crimp 2 in. (5 cm) from the first crimp. Go back through the crimp, leaving a small loop, and crimp. Trim the wire ends and cover the crimps with crimp covers.

For a double-strand component, string a crimp tube over both ends of a 13-in. (33 cm) length of wire. Place the crimp tube toward the fold in the center of the wire, leaving a small wire loop. Crimp the crimp tube and cover with a crimp cover. String beads and crimp tubes as directed below. String a crimp tube over both wire ends **[a]**. Place the final crimp tube 2 in. from the first crimp cover. Pass one end of the wire back through the crimp tube, leaving a small wire loop **[b]**. Crimp the crimp tube. Trim the wire ends. Cover the crimp tube with a crimp cover **[c]**.

a. double-strand: Use bronze wire. On one wire, string four bronze 11º seed beads and a 2 x 2 crimp tube. Repeat twice, and end with four bronze 11ºs. On the other wire, string seven brown 11ºs, a crimp, and seven brown 11ºs. Space the strung crimps evenly along the two wires and crimp all tubes. Cover each crimp with a crimp cover. Set aside **[d]**.

b. single strand: On bronze wire, string six bronze 11º seed beads and a crimp tube. Repeat twice. Space the strung crimps evenly along the wire and crimp all tubes. Cover each crimp with a crimp cover. Set aside.

c. double strand: Use peridot wire. On one wire, string four chartreuse 11º seed beads and a crimp tube. Repeat twice. String four chartreuse 11ºs. On the other wire, string six chartreuse 11ºs and a crimp tube. Repeat. String six chartreuse 11ºs. Space the strung crimps evenly along the two wires and crimp all tubes. Cover each crimp with a crimp cover. Set aside.

d. single strand: On peridot wire, string four chartreuse 11º seed beads and a crimp tube. Repeat twice. String four chartreuse 11ºs. Space the strung crimp tubes evenly along the wire and crimp all tubes. Cover each crimp tube with a crimp cover. Set aside.

e. single strand: On black onyx wire, string seven black 11º seed beads and a crimp tube. String seven black 11ºs. Space the crimp tube evenly along the wire and crimp. Cover the crimp tube with a crimp cover. Set aside.

f. single strand: On black onyx wire, string five black 11º seed beads and a crimp tube. Repeat twice. String five black 11ºs. Space the strung crimp tubes evenly along the wire and crimp all tubes. Cover each crimp tube with a crimp cover. Set aside.

g. double strand: On bronze wire, string five brown 11º seed beads and a crimp tube. Repeat. String five brown 11ºs. On the other end of the wire, string five bronze 11ºs and a crimp tube. Repeat. String five bronze 11ºs. Space the strung crimp tubes evenly along the two wires and crimp all tubes.

Cover each crimp tube with a crimp cover. Set aside.

h. single strand: On bronze wire, string seven bronze 11º seed beads and a crimp tube. String seven bronze 11ºs. Space the crimp evenly along the wire and crimp. Cover with a crimp cover. Set aside.

i. single strand: On peridot wire, string seven chartreuse 11º seed beads and a crimp tube. String seven chartreuse 11ºs. Space the strung crimp evenly along the wire and crimp. Cover the crimp with a crimp cover. Set aside.

j. single strand: On peridot wire, string five chartreuse 11º seed beads and a crimp tube. Repeat twice. String five chartreuse 11ºs. Space the strung crimps evenly along the wire and crimp all tubes. Cover each crimp with a crimp cover. Set aside.

k. double strand: On one end of black onyx wire, string seven black 11º seed beads, a crimp tube, and seven black 11ºs. On the other end, string four black 11ºs and a crimp. Repeat once. String four black 11ºs. Space the strung crimps evenly along the two wires and crimp all tubes. Cover each crimp with a crimp cover. Set aside.

l. single strand: On black onyx wire, string six black 11º seed beads and a crimp tube. Repeat. String six black 11ºs. Space the strung crimp tubes evenly along the wire and crimp all tubes. Cover each crimp tube with a crimp cover. Set aside.

m. double strand: On one end of bronze wire, string seven bronze 11º seed beads, a crimp tube, and seven bronze seed beads. On the other end string five bronze 11ºs and a crimp tube. Repeat. String five bronze 11ºs. Space the strung crimps evenly along the two wires and crimp all tubes. Cover each crimp tube with a crimp cover. Set aside.

n. single strand: On bronze wire, string six brown 11º seed beads and a crimp tube. Repeat. String six brown 11ºs. Space the strung crimp tubes evenly along the wire and crimp all tubes. Cover each crimp tube with a crimp cover. Set aside.

o. double strand: On one end of black onyx wire, string five black 11º seed beads and a crimp tube. Repeat. String five black 11ºs. On the other end, string six black 11ºs, a crimp tube, and six black 11ºs. Space the strung crimp tubes evenly along the two wires and crimp all tubes. Cover each crimp with a crimp cover. Set aside.

p. single strand: On black onyx wire, string four black 11º seed beads and a crimp tube. Repeat twice. String four black 11ºs. Space the strung crimp tubes evenly

along the wire and crimp all tubes. Cover each crimp tube with a crimp cover. Set aside.

q. double strand: On one end of peridot wire, string seven chartreuse 11º seed beads, a crimp tube, and seven chartreuse 11ºs. On the other end, string five chartreuse 11ºs and a crimp tube. Repeat twice. String five chartreuse 11ºs. Space the strung crimp tubes evenly along the two wires and crimp all tubes. Cover each crimp tube with a crimp cover. Set aside.

r. single strand: On peridot wire, string seven chartreuse 11º seed beads, a crimp tube, and seven chartreuse 11ºs. Space the strung crimp tube evenly along the wire and crimp. Cover the crimp tube with a crimp cover. Set aside.

s. single strand: On bronze wire, string seven brown 11º seed beads, a crimp tube, and string seven brown 11ºs. Space the crimp tube evenly along the wire and crimp. Cover the crimp tube with a crimp cover. Set aside.

t. single strand: On bronze wire, string five bronze 11º seed beads and a crimp tube. Repeat twice. String five bronze 11ºs. Space the strung crimp tubes evenly along the wire and crimp all tubes. Cover each crimp tube with a crimp cover. Set aside.

*String a pattern of beads and
the end loops of the components
as if you're putting rungs on a ladder.*

Assemble the bracelet

1 Arrange the components on your work space in the order in which they were made.

2 Use 10 in. (25 cm) of bronze beading wire to string a crimp tube and a clasp half. Go back through the tube and crimp. Cover the crimp with a crimp cover. String a brown matte metallic 11º, a 6 mm pearl, an 11º, a casbah, an 11º, **component a**, an 11º, and **component b**. String an 11º, an 8 mm pearl, an 11º, **component c**, an 11º, and **component d**. String an 11º, a casbah, an 11º, **component e**, an 11º, and **component f**. String an 11º, an 8 mm pearl, an 11º, **component g**, an 11º, and **component h**. String an 11º, a casbah, an 11º, **component i**, an 11º, and **component j**. String an 11º, an 8 mm pearl, an 11º, **component k**, an 11º, and **component l**. String an 11º, a casbah, an 11º, **component m**, an 11º, and **component n**. String an 11º, an 8 mm pearl, an 11º, **component o**, an 11º, and **component p**. String an 11º, a casbah, an 11º, **component q**, an 11º, and **component r**. String an 11º, an 8 mm pearl, an 11º, **component s**, an 11º, **component t**, an 11º, a casbah, an 11º, a 6 mm pearl, an 11º, a crimp tube, and the other clasp half. Go back through the tube and crimp. Cover with a crimp cover.

3 Repeat Step 2 using the other clasp and stringing the other ends of all the components.

Carnival

Sometimes a surprising color combination is just the ticket. Showcase the beading wire color by anchoring beads in place with a crimp on each side.

materials

- Beading Wire (.019):
  8 in. (20 cm) red jasper
- **2** 8 mm tanzanite crystal bicones
- **4** 6 mm tanzanite crystal bicones
- **4** 8º burnt sienna over opaque yellow-orange seed beads
- **12** 11º burnt sienna over opaque yellow-orange seed beads
- **4** 2 x 2 mm sterling silver crimp tubes
- **12** 1 x 1 mm sterling silver crimp tubes
- **4** 3 mm sterling silver crimp covers
- pair of sterling silver earring wires

tools

- chainnose pliers
- crimping pliers
- micro crimping pliers
- wire cutters

Finished Size:
1⅝ in. (4.1 cm)

a

c

b

d

e

1 Center a 1 x 1 mm crimp tube, an 11º seed bead, an 8º seed bead, an 8 mm crystal, an 8º, an 11º, and a 1 x 1 mm crimp on a 4-in. (10 cm) piece of beading wire. Use micro crimping pliers to crimp the tubes on both sides of the beads **[a]**.

2 On one end of the wire, string a 1 x 1 mm crimp, an 11º, a 6 mm, an 11º, and a 1 x 1 mm crimp. Place the first crimp strung ½ in. (1.3 cm) from the previous crimped tube, and crimp. Snug the beads and crimp the remaining tube. Repeat on the other end of the wire **[b, c]**.

3 On one end of the wire, string two 2 x 2 mm crimp tubes. With the other end of the wire, pass through the tubes in the opposite direction. Adjust the wires so there is about ¼ in. (6 mm) between the last 1 x 1 mm crimp and the 2 x 2 mm crimp on both sides of the 2 x 2 mm crimps and that the ring is about 26 mm. Crimp both 2 x 2 mm crimps and cover each tube with a crimp cover **[d, e]**.

4 Use chainnose pliers to attach an earring wire to the ring between the two crimp covers.

5 Make a second earring.

Dream Baby

Create this fabulous look by layering complementary colors. Mix crystals, seed beads and beading wire in three different colors. An ornamental clasp can become part of the design by moving it to the side.

materials

- Beading Wire (.019):
  24 in. (61 cm) amethyst
  24 in. garnet
  35 in. (89 cm) pink tourmaline
- 15 x 21 mm pewter faerie/joy pendant
- **9** 6 mm tanzanite bicone crystals
- **9** 6 mm ruby bicone crystals
- **9** 6 mm rose bicone crystals
- **8** 4 mm tanzanite bicone crystals
- **8** 4 mm ruby bicone crystals
- **8** 4 mm rose bicone crystals
- **108** 15º purple-lined transparent amethyst seed beads
- **108** 15º opaque magenta seed beads
- **339** 14º or 15º desert dust seed beads
- **54** 1 x 1 mm sterling silver crimp tubes
- **2** 2 x 2 mm sterling silver crimp tubes
- **2** 3 x 3 mm sterling silver crimp tubes
- **2** 13 x 46 mm sterling silver leaf hook-and-eye clasps

tools

- crimping pliers
- micro crimping pliers
- mighty crimping pliers
- wire cutters
- bead stoppers

Finished Size: 20 in. (51 cm)

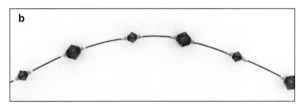

a

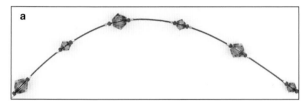

b

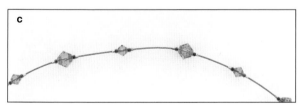

c

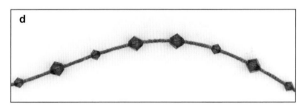

d

1 Place a bead stopper on one end of a 12-in. (30 cm) length of amethyst wire. String a 1 x 1 mm crimp tube, a magenta 15º seed bead, a tanzanite 6 mm, a magenta 15º, two 1 x 1 mm crimps, a magenta 15º, a tanzanite 4 mm, a magenta 15º, and a 1 x 1 mm crimp. Repeat three times. String a 1 x 1 mm crimp, a magenta 15º, a tanzanite 6 mm, a magenta 15º, and a 1 x 1 mm crimp. Place a bead stopper on the wire end.

2 Remove the first bead stopper and place the first crimp tube about 2 in. (5 cm) from the end of the wire. Crimp with micro

crimping pliers. Snug the beads and crimp the next crimp.

3 Place a crimp about ½ in. (1.3 cm) from the previous crimp, and crimp with micro crimping pliers. Snug the beads and crimp the next tube. Repeat seven times. Set aside **[a]**.

4 Repeat steps 1–3 with garnet wire, desert dust 14ºs, and ruby crystals. Set aside **[b]**.

5 Repeat Steps 1–3 with pink tourmaline wire, amethyst 15º seed beads, and rose crystals. Set aside **[c]**.

6 Place a bead stopper on one end of a 12-in. (30 cm) length of amethyst wire. String 10 amethyst 15º seed beads, a ruby 4 mm, 10 amethyst 15ºs, and a ruby 6 mm. Repeat. String 10 amethyst 15ºs, a ruby 6 mm, 10 amethyst 15ºs, and a ruby 4 mm. Repeat. String 10 amethyst 15ºs. Place a bead stopper on the wire end. Set aside **[d]**.

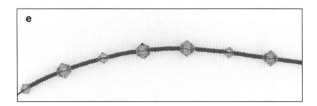

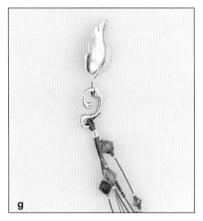

7 Repeat Step 6 using garnet wire, magenta 15º seed beads, and rose crystals **[e]**.

8 Place a bead stopper on one end of a 12-in. length of pink tourmaline wire. String 10 desert dust 14º seed beads, a tanzanite 4 mm, 10 desert dust 14ºs, and a tanzanite 6 mm. Repeat. String the pewter pendant. String 10 desert dust 14ºs, a tanzanite 6 mm, 10 desert dust 14ºs, and a tanzanite 4 mm. Repeat. String 10 desert dust 14ºs. Place a bead stopper on the wire end and set aside **[f]**.

9 Remove one bead stopper from every wire. String a 3 x 3 mm crimp tube and the hook half of one clasp over all six wires. Adjust the wires as necessary so that they lie nicely together and there is about 4 in. between the crimp tube and the pendant. Pass the wires back through the tube and crimp, using mighty crimping pliers **[g]**.

10 Repeat Step 9 on the other end, using the hook half of the second clasp.

11 On 11 in. of pink tourmaline wire, string one 2 x 2 mm crimp tube, six desert dust 14º seed beads, the eye half of one clasp, and six desert dust 14ºs. Pass the wire back through the tube and crimp using crimping pliers. String 207 desert dust 14ºs, a 2 x 2 mm crimp, six desert dust 14ºs, the eye half of the second clasp, and six desert dust 14ºs. Pass the wire back through the tube and crimp using crimping pliers **[h]**.

Keep the multi-strand action front and center, and leave a single strand behind the neck. The side clasps appear to be integrated design elements: Form and function!

Fire and Rain

In this necklace, replace the clear cord commonly found in illusion jewelry with a colorful strand of beading wire. Simple dangles in various lengths complete this beautiful design.

materials

- Beading Wire (.019): 50 in. (1.3 m) turquoise
- **5** 8 mm topaz crystal bicones
- **5** 6 mm pacific opal crystal bicones
- **4** 6 mm topaz crystal bicones
- **9** 4 mm pacific opal crystal bicones
- **4** 4 mm topaz crystal bicones
- **21** 8º opaque light aqua seed beads
- **15** 11º opaque light aqua seed beads
- **131** 15º opaque light aqua seed beads
- 8 x 14 mm sterling silver filigree box clasp with attached 3 mm jump rings
- **30** 2 x 2 mm sterling silver crimp tubes

tools

- crimping pliers
- wire cutters

Finished Size: 17½ in. (44.5 cm)

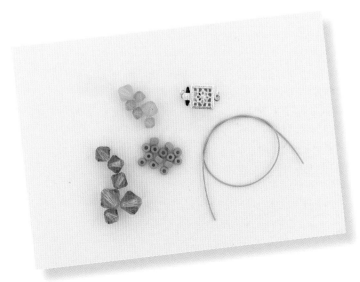

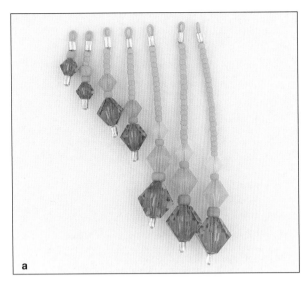

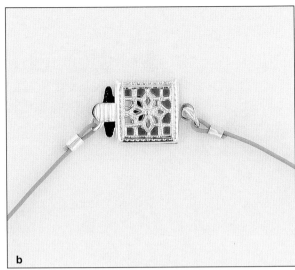

1 Cut the beading wire into eight 2-in. (5 cm) pieces, five 3-in. (7.6 cm) pieces, and one 19-in. (48 cm) piece.

2 On a 2-in. piece of beading wire, string a crimp tube. Go back through the tube, forming a loop large enough to fit over the .019 diameter beading wire, and crimp. Repeat with the 2- and 3-in. wire pieces to make eight short wires and five long wires.

Create dangles in steps 3–9 as shown **[a]**.

3 On a short wire, string an 11º seed bead, a 4 mm topaz crystal, and a crimp tube. Snug the beads and crimp the crimp tube for a dangle about ½-in. (1.3 cm) long. Repeat to make two ½-in. dangles.

4 On a short wire, string three 15º seed beads, an 8º seed bead, an 11º seed bead, a 4 mm topaz crystal, and a crimp tube. Snug the bead and crimp the tube for a ¾-in. (1.9 cm) dangle. Repeat to make two ¾-in. dangles.

5 On a short wire, string five 15º seed beads, a 4 mm pacific opal crystal, an 11º seed bead, a 6 mm topaz crystal, and a crimp tube. Snug the beads and crimp the crimp tube for a ⅞-in. (2.2 cm) dangle. Repeat to make two ⅞-in. dangles.

6 On a short wire, string 10 15º seed beads, a 4 mm pacific opal crystal, an 11º seed bead, a 6 mm topaz crystal, and a crimp tube. Snug the beads and crimp the crimp tube for a 1⅛-in. (2.9 cm) dangle. Repeat to make two 1⅛-in. dangles.

7 On a long wire, string 15 15º seed beads, a 4 mm pacific opal crystal, an 11º seed bead, a 6 mm pacific opal crystal, an 8º seed bead, an 8 mm topaz crystal, and a crimp tube. Snug the beads and crimp the crimp tube for a 1¾-in. (4.4 cm) dangle. Repeat to make two 1¾-in. dangles.

8 On a long wire, string 20 15º seed beads, a 4 mm pacific opal crystal, an 11º seed bead, a 6 mm pacific opal crystal, an 8º seed bead, an 8 mm topaz crystal, and a crimp tube. Snug the beads and crimp the crimp tube for a 1⅞-in. (4.8 cm) dangle. Repeat to make two 1⅞-in. dangles.

9 On a long wire, string 23 15º seed beads, a pacific opal 4 mm crystal, an 11º seed bead, a 6 mm pacific opal crystal, an 8º seed bead, an 8 mm topaz crystal, and a crimp tube. Snug the beads and crimp the crimp tube for a 2⅛-in. (5.4 cm) dangle.

10 On the 19-in. wire, string a crimp tube, a 15º seed bead, a 11º seed bead, a 8º seed bead, a ½-in. dangle, an 8º, a ¾-in. dangle, an 8º, a ⅞-in. dangle, an 8º, a 1⅛-in. dangle, an 8º, a 1¾-in. dangle, an 8º, a 1⅞-in. dangle, an 8º, the 2⅛-in. dangle, an 8º, a 1⅞-in. dangle, an 8º, a 1¾-in. dangle, an 8º, a 1⅛-in. dangle, an 8º, a ⅞-in. dangle, an 8º, a ¾-in. dangle, an 8º, a ½-in. dangle, an 8º, an 11º, a 15º, and a crimp tube to the center of the wire. Crimp the first crimp tube strung. Snug the beads and crimp the second crimp tube.

11 On one end of the beading wire, string a crimp tube and the jump ring on one half of the clasp. Go back through the tube, adjust the wire so that there is 7⅜ in. between the crimp tubes, and crimp. Repeat for the other end of the necklace, using the other clasp half **[b]**.

Chapter 3

KNITTING
SPOOL

Knitting with beading wire is easy when you use a spool. Use a single strand of wire to make a "cage" and feature other beads and wires within it; braid long lengths of wire knitted with matching seed beads for a thick wrap bracelet or belt; knit many strands of wires together and string with any variation of beads to form numerous weaves and designs; and so much more. Colored beading wire is the perfect medium for these projects because it is strong enough to be knitted and the different colors provide a lovely palette to work with. For these projects, do not cut any wire from the spools until instructed to do so. You'll knit the beading wire directly from the wire spools onto the knitting spool.

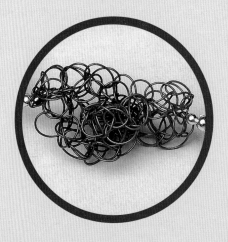

Long and Winding Road

Three long lengths of knitted wire in blue topaz, green emerald, and black onyx, with randomly-placed matching seed beads, are braided together to form this sweet, funky, and stretchy double-wrap cuff.

materials

- Beading Wire (.019):
  100 ft. (30.5 m) spool blue topaz
  100 ft. spool black onyx
  100 ft. spool green emerald
- 5 g 11º aqua dark matte AB seed beads
- 5 g 11º black matte opaque seed beads
- 5 g 11º matte transparent olive green seed beads
- **2** 20 x 23 mm sterling silver textured cones
- **2** 3 x 3 mm sterling silver crimp tubes
- 12 x 17 mm sterling silver toggle clasp

tools

- mighty crimping pliers
- wire cutters
- 3-peg knitting spool with stylus
- bead stoppers

Finished Size: 14 in. (36 cm)

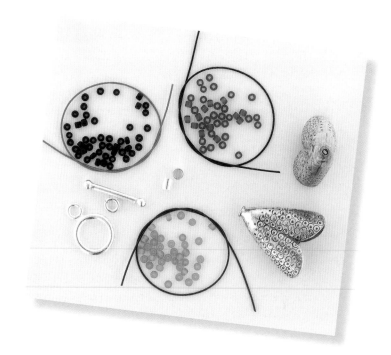

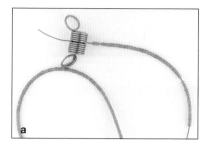

a

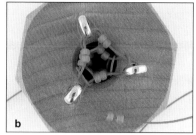

b

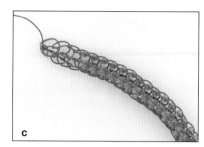

c

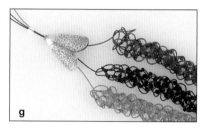

d

e

f

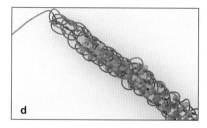

g

h

i

1 String about 18 in. (46 cm) of aqua 11º seed beads on the blue wire. Place a bead stopper on the end of the wire **[a]**.

2 Move the 11ºs about 2 ft. (61 cm) down the wire toward the spool. Remove the bead stopper. Pass the end of the wire through the hole in the knitting spool, from top to bottom. Replace the bead stopper.

3 Begin knitting, following Knitting Spool 101 instructions for single-wrap knitting (see page 20). Knit three complete rounds.

4 Prior to knitting the next stitch, slide two 11ºs up the wire between the peg you are about to knit a stitch on and the next peg. Knit one stitch. Repeat for 12 in. (30 cm), including two 11ºs in each stitch **[b]**.

5 Knit without beads for two complete rounds. Cut the wire 10 in. (25 cm) from

the last peg stitched. Working around the spool, pass the wire ends through every wire loop on the spool. Once the wire ends have passed through a wire loop, carefully remove the wire loop from the knitting spool. Repeat for all three pegs, then carefully pull the knitted cord out of the knitting spool. Pull tightly on the end of the knitted cord, tightening the last few stitches as much as possible **[c]**.

6 Use your fingers to crunch the stitches of the knitted cord together so the seed beads move around and the wire stitches become uneven and messy looking **[d]**.

7 Repeat Steps 1–6 using the black wire and black 11º seed beads **[e]**.

8 Repeat Steps 1–6 using the green wire and green 11º seed beads **[f]**.

9 Use one end of all three knitted cords to string a cone (wide end first), a crimp tube **[g]**, and the ring half of the clasp. Arrange the knitted cords so that the turquoise blue topaz cord is on the left, the black onyx cord in the middle, and the green emerald cord on the right. Pull the wire ends so that the three knitted cords fit snugly inside the cone. Pass all three wire ends back through the tube **[h]**. Crimp the crimp tube.

10 Braid the three knitted cords together **[i]** until you reach the end of the cords. Repeat Step 9, substituting the bar half of the clasp.

To wear, wrap the bracelet twice around your wrist.

Burlesque

Knit warm shades of beading wire in garnet, imperial topaz, and red jasper together with assorted brass beads in this comforting bracelet. Some brass beads are strung on one strand of wire and some are strung on all three strands, so they look randomly placed but blend perfectly into the knit.

materials
- Beading Wire (.019):
  30-ft. (9.2 m) spool garnet
  30-ft. spool imperial topaz
  30-ft. spool red jasper
- **30** 3 mm brass cubes
- **30** 3 mm brass tubes
- **40** 3 mm brass fluted rounds
- **2** 16 x 19 mm brass magnolia leaf
  bead caps
- **2** 3 mm sterling silver crimp tubes
- 16 x 25 mm brass leaf toggle clasp

tools
- mighty crimping pliers
- wire cutters
- 5-pin knitting spool with stylus
- bead stoppers

Finished Size: 7¼ in.

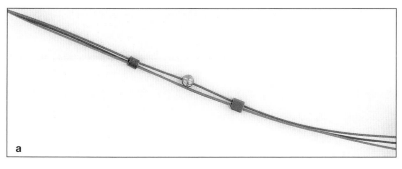

a

b

c

d

1 Over the ends of all three beading wires, string a brass cube. On the red jasper wire, string a fluted round. Over all three wires, string a brass tube. On the red jasper wire, string a fluted round **[a]**. Repeat ten times, unwinding more wire from the spools and pushing beads down the wire as necessary.

2 Over all three beading wires, string a brass cube. On the red jasper wire, string a fluted round. Over all three wires, string a brass tube. Repeat 20 times, unwinding more wire from the spools and pushing beads down the wire as necessary.

3 Pass the ends of the wires through the hole in the knitting spool, from top to bottom. Place a bead stopper on the ends of the wires.

4 Using the wires together as one, begin knitting, following Knitting Spool 101 instructions for single-wrap knitting (see page 20). Knit three complete rounds.

5 Prior to knitting the next stitch, slide one bead up the wire between the peg you are about to knit a stitch on and the next peg. Knit two stitches.

6 Repeat Step 5, adding one bead to every other stitch, until the knitted cord is 6¼ in. (15.9 cm).

7 Cut all three wires 10 in. (25 cm) from the last peg stitched. Working around the spool, pass the wire ends through every wire loop on the spool. Once the wire ends have passed through a wire loop, carefully remove the wire loop from the knitting spool. Repeat for all four pegs, then carefully pull the knitted cord out of the knitting spool. Pull tightly on the end of the knitted cord, tightening the last few stitches as much as possible.

8 Carefully open the petals of a magnolia leaf bead cap until flat. Use all three wire ends to string a crimp tube, the flat bead cap (inside out), and the ring half of the clasp. Go back through the bead cap and the crimp tube **[b]**.

9 Snug the crimp tube and bead cap as close to the end of the knitted cord as possible, and crimp **[c]**. Trim the wire ends. Carefully fold the petals of the bead cap down around the end of the knitted cord **[d]**.

10 Remove the bead stopper from the other ends of the wires. Repeat Step 8, using the bar half of the clasp and leaving a loop of wire large enough to allow the bar half of the clasp to fit through the ring half of the clasp.

Moonstruck

Bright, citrusy colors perfectly match the enameled pendant in this necklace. Black beads woven through the knitted section with black beading wire unify the piece. The beading wire colors swirl together in the knit in the same way as in the pendant, intensifying the effect.

materials

- Beading Wire (.019):
  30-ft. (9.2 m) spool of citrine
  30-ft. spool yellow lemon quartz
  30-ft. spool chrysoprase
  18 in. (46 cm) black onyx
- 118 in. (3.0 m) 22-gauge Non-Tarnish Silver craft wire
- 24 x 50 mm green/orange/yellow/black enameled glass pendant with attached 6 x 11 mm jump ring
- **16** 5 x 7 mm black Czech pressed-glass teardrops
- **12** 10 mm black Czech pressed-glass rounds
- **2** 3 x 3 mm sterling silver crimp tubes
- **2** 4 mm sterling silver crimp covers
- 13 x 37 mm sterling silver hook-and-eye clasp

tools

- chainnose pliers
- roundnose pliers
- needlenose pliers
- wire cutters
- 3-peg knitting spool with stylus
- Speeder Beader

Finished Size: 19¼ in.

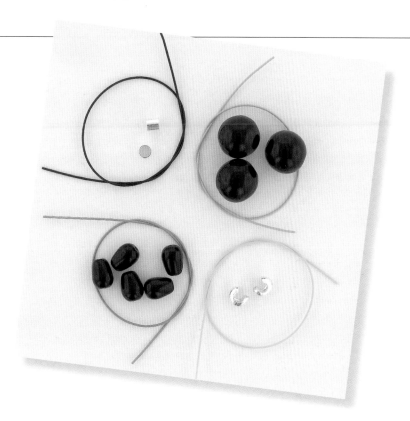

1 Pass the ends of the citrine, yellow lemon quartz, and chrysoprase beading wires through the hole in the knitting spool, from top to bottom.

2 Using the wires together as one, begin knitting, following Knitting Spool 101 instructions for single-wrap knitting (page 20), making sure to keep a loose tension. Knit for 9 in. (23 cm).

3 Cut all three wires 10 in. (25 cm) from the last peg stitched. Working around the spool, pass the wire ends through every wire loop on the spool. Once the wire ends have passed through a wire loop, carefully remove the wire loop from the knitting spool. Repeat for all four pegs, then carefully pull the knitted cord out of the knitting spool. Pull tightly on the end of the knitted cord, tightening the last few stitches as much as possible. Place a bead stopper on the ends of the wires.

4 Place one end of the black wire inside the channel of a Speeder Beader. Beginning about ¾ in. (1.9 cm) from one end of the knitted cord, pass the Speeder Beader through the center of the cord. *Remove the Speeder Beader and string a teardrop (narrow end first). Put the wire back into the Speeder Beader and go back through the center of the knitted cord. Pass from the back of the cord to the front. Repeat from * seven times, for a total of eight teardrops stitched to the cord **[a]**. The last bead stitched should be just before the center of the knitted cord.

5 Repeat Step 4, stringing the teardrops wide end first for the remaining half.

6 Remove the bead stopper from one end of the knitted cord. String a crimp tube over all four beading wire ends. Snug the crimp tube as close to the end of the knitted cord as possible. Go back through the tube, leaving a small loop of wires **[b]**.

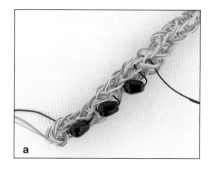

a

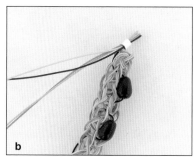

b

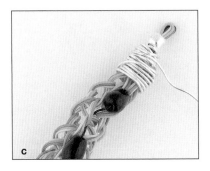

7 Crimp the tube and cover with a crimp cover. Use 16 in. (41 cm) of 22-gauge wire to wrap around the end of the knitted cord. Begin just after the crimp cover and continue for ¾ in. (1.9 cm) toward the center of the cord. Repeat, using a second 16-in. wire to make the hand-wrapped bead cap bulkier **[c]**.

8 Make a wrapped loop with 4½ in. (11.4 cm) of 22-gauge wire. String a pressed-glass round and make the first half of a wrapped loop above the bead. Connect the wire loop to the loop formed in Step 6 and complete the wraps **[d]**.

9 Make the first half of a wrapped loop with 4½ in. of 22-gauge wire. Connect it to the loop formed in Step 8 and complete the wraps. String a pressed-glass round and make a wrapped loop. Repeat to connect six beaded links. Before completing the wraps on the last link, attach half the clasp. Complete the wraps.

10 Repeat Steps 6–9 on the other end of the necklace.

11 Use the jump ring to attach the pendant to the center of the knitted cord **[e]**.

The Speeder Beader's rigid needle makes it much easier to guide the beading wire through the knitted base. For a closer view of this tool, turn to page 22.

Heart of Stone

The color palette of these gorgeous earrings, with gemstones and glass beads caged inside an open knit of red jasper beading wire, is rich and earthy. Though the beads look like they're just floating in the wire knit, they're actually strung on fluorite beading wire that perfectly complements the beads. Wire ends don't seem to exist in these hoops; they're crimped on either side of simple lever-back earrings.

materials

- Beading Wire (.019):
  30-ft. (9.2 m) spool red jasper
  18 in. (46 cm) fluorite
- **4** 8 mm amber/matte clear fire-polished rounds
- **4** 8 x 6 mm mottled green Czech pressed-glass diamond cubes
- **10** 6 mm old rose fire-polished rounds
- **4** 6 mm turquoise rounds
- **4** 11 mm sterling silver textured bullet-end bead caps
- **2** 2 x 2 mm sterling silver crimp tubes
- **2** 3 mm sterling silver crimp covers
- pair of sterling silver leverback earring wires

tools

- crimping pliers
- wire cutters
- 4-peg knitting spool

Finished Size: 2⅛ in. (5.4 cm)

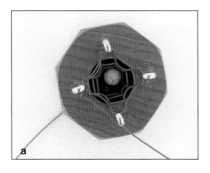

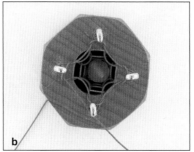

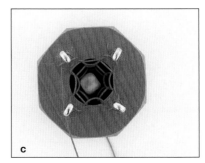

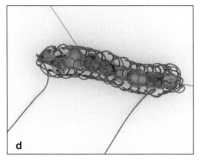

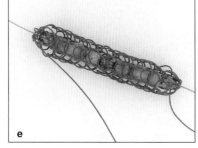

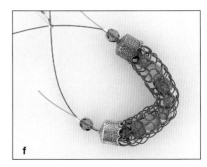

1 Pass the end of the red jasper beading wire through the hole in the knitting spool, from top to bottom. Attach a bead stopper to the end of the wire.

2 Knit six complete rounds, following Knitting Spool 101 instructions for single-wrap knitting (see page 20).

3 Drop an old rose round into the knitted tube. Continue knitting. Drop a turquoise round into the tube. Continue knitting **[a]**.

4 Drop an amber round into the tube. Continue knitting **[b]**.

5 Drop a green cube into the tube. Continue knitting **[c]**.

6 Repeat Steps 3–5. Drop an old rose round into the tube. Knit until the bead is completely inside the knitting spool.

7 Cut the wire 10 in. (25 cm) from the last peg stitched. Working around the spool,

pass the wire ends through every wire loop on the spool. Once the wire ends have passed through a loop, carefully remove the loop from the knitting spool. Repeat for all four pegs, then carefully pull the knitted cord out of the knitting spool. Pull tightly on the end of the knitted cord, tightening the last few stitches as much as possible.

8 Cut a 9-in. (23 cm) length of fluorite wire, and pass the end through the end of the knitted cord. Pass it through the bead holes, one at a time, all the way through the knitted cord **[d, e]**.

9 On one end of the red jasper and fluorite wires, string a bead cap (wide end first), an old rose round, and a crimp tube. Repeat on the other ends of the wires.

10 String an earring wire on one end of the red jasper wire. Pass the other end of the red jasper wire through the earring wire in the opposite direction **[f]**.

11 String each end of the red jasper wire back through the crimp tube at the ends of the wire. Pull the wire ends tight, making sure the bead caps are snug against the knitted cord, and crimp **[g]**.

12 Trim the wire ends and cover each crimp tube with a crimp cover **[h]**.

13 Make a second earring.

Silkwood

Three colors of beading wire, each strung with matching fire-polished rounds, are knitted together in this bangle. This beautiful blend of pastel colors has one bead worked into each stitch, which gives it a fabulous density. The light and dark shades make this bracelet a treat for the eyes.

materials

- Beading Wire (.019):
  30-ft. (9.2 m) spool peridot
  30-ft. spool garnet
  30-ft. spool tanzanite
- 8-in. (20 cm) strand 4 mm milky green fire-polished rounds
- 8-in. strand 4 mm garnet-and-gray fire-polished rounds
- 8-in. strand 4 mm milky blue fire-polished rounds
- **2** 10 x 20 mm Thai silver hammered cones
- **2** 3 x 3 mm sterling silver crimp tubes
- **2** 4 mm sterling silver crimp covers
- 20 x 22 mm Thai silver hammered toggle clasp

tools

- wire cutters
- mighty crimping pliers
- 4-peg knitting spool with stylus
- bead stoppers

Finished Size: 8¾ in. (22.2 cm)

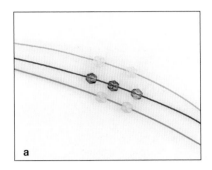

a

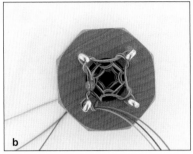

b

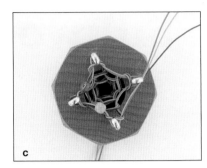

c

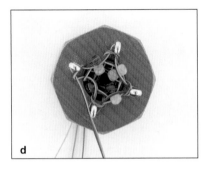

d

1 On the peridot beading wire, string all the milky green fire-polished rounds. On the garnet wire, string all the garnet-and-gray fire-polished rounds. On the tanzanite wire, string all the milky blue fire-polished rounds **[a]**.

2 Pass the ends of the wires through the hole in the knitting spool, from top to bottom. Attach a bead stopper to the ends of the wires.

3 Using the wires together as one, begin knitting, following Knitting Spool 101 instructions for single-wrap knitting (see page 20). Knit three complete rounds.

4 Prior to knitting the next stitch, slide one garnet-and-gray bead up the wire between the peg you are about to knit a stitch on and the next peg. Knit one stitch **[b]**.

5 Prior to knitting the next stitch, slide one milky blue bead up the wire between the peg you are about to knit a stitch on and the next peg. Knit one stitch **[c]**.

6 Prior to knitting the next stitch, slide one milky green bead up the wire between the peg you are about to knit a stitch on and the next peg. Knit one stitch.

7 Repeat Steps 4–6 for 6 in. (15 cm) or until all beads are incorporated into the knitted cord **[d]**.

8 Knit without beads for two complete rounds. Cut all three wires 10 in. (25 cm) from the last peg stitched. Working around the spool, pass the wire ends through every wire loop on the spool. Once the wire ends have passed through a wire loop, carefully remove the wire loop from the knitting spool. Repeat for all four pegs, then carefully pull the knitted cord out of the knitting spool. Pull tightly on the end of the knitted cord, tightening the last few stitches as much as possible.

9 Over all three wire ends, string a cone, a crimp tube, and one half of the clasp. Snug the cone tightly onto the end of the knitted cord. Go back through the tube and crimp. Trim wire ends. Cover the crimp tube with a crimp cover.

10 Remove the bead stopper from the other end of the knitted cord. Repeat Step 9, attaching the wire to the other half of the clasp.

Caesar's Palace

This elegant necklace is made of short lengths of knitted beading wire in neutral colors, crimped and linked together like chain. Loosely knit, bead-free links make this piece incredibly lightweight, even though it looks luxuriously heavy. The silver clasp and crimp findings add to the elegant color-scheme.

materials
- Beading Wire (.019):
  30-ft. (9.2 m) spool antique brass
  30-ft. spool copper
  30-ft. spool bronze
  30-ft. spool champagne
- **25** 2 x 2 mm sterling silver crimp tubes
- **7** 4 mm sterling silver crimp covers
- **18** 3 mm sterling silver crimp covers
- 13 x 46 mm sterling silver leaf hook-and-eye clasp

tools
- crimping pliers
- wire cutters
- 3-peg knitting spool with stylus

Finished Size: 18¾ in. (47.6 cm)

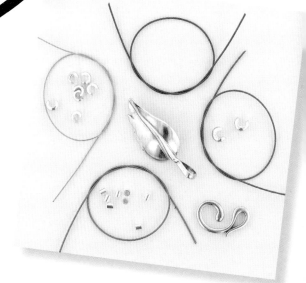

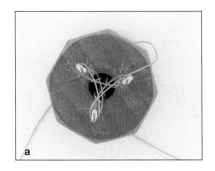

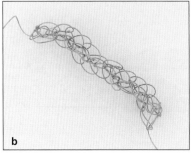

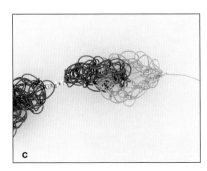

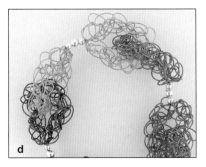

Feeling bold? Try this design with wire in jewel tones or primary colors for a fresh look.

1 Use the champagne beading wire and the knitting spool to knit a 3–3½-in. (7.6–8.9 cm) cord, following Knitting Spool 101 instructions for double-wrap knitting (see page 21) **[a]**.

2 Cut the wire 10 in. (25 cm) from the last peg stitched. Working around the spool, pass the wire ends through every wire loop on the spool. Once the wire ends have passed through a wire loop, carefully remove the loop from the knitting spool. Repeat for all three pegs, then carefully pull the knitted cord out of the knitting spool. Pull tightly on the end of the knitted cord, tightening the last few stitches as much as possible. Set aside **[b]**.

3 Repeat Steps 1 and 2 three times, for a total of four champagne knitted cords.

4 Use antique brass beading wire to repeat Steps 1 and 2 four times, for a total of four antique brass knitted cords.

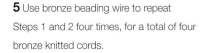

5 Use bronze beading wire to repeat Steps 1 and 2 four times, for a total of four bronze knitted cords.

6 Use copper beading wire to repeat Steps 1 and 2 four times, for a total of four copper knitted cords.

7 String a crimp tube over both ends of a copper knitted cord. Snug the crimp to the ends of the cord and crimp. Cut one wire end. Cover the crimp with a crimp cover. Use the remaining wire end to string a crimp tube and the hook half of the clasp. Go back through the tube and crimp. Cover with a 3 mm crimp cover.

8 Pass an antique brass knitted cord through the knitted wire loop formed in the previous step. String a crimp tube over both ends of the antique brass cord. Snug the crimp tube to the ends of the cord and crimp. Cut one wire end. Cover the crimp with a 3 mm crimp cover. Set aside.

9 String a crimp tube over an antique brass knitted cord. Snug the crimp tube to the ends of the cord and crimp. Cut one wire end. Cover the crimp with a 3 mm crimp cover. String a crimp over the remaining wire end. Pass the remaining wire from Step 8 through the crimp tube in the opposite direction. Pull the wire ends until there is about 1 mm of wire remaining on

both sides of the crimp tube, and crimp. Cover the crimp with a 4 mm crimp cover.

10 Repeat Steps 8 and 9 using champagne cords **[c]**.

11 Repeat Steps 8 and 9 using bronze cords.

12 Repeat Steps 8 and 9 using copper cords.

13 Repeat Steps 8 and 9.

14 Repeat Steps 8 and 9 using champagne cords.

15 Repeat Steps 8 and 9 using bronze cords **[d]**.

16 Repeat Step 8 using a copper cord. Use the remaining wire end to string a crimp tube and the eye/leaf half of the clasp. Go back through the tube and crimp. Cover with a 3 mm crimp cover.

Chapter 4

SCULPTURAL

Show your colors by forming shapes using colored beading wire. Strategically placed crimps can create all sorts of neat outlines, such as stars, circles, and ovals. The shapes can be linked, made big or small, and in some cases, even stand all on their own as a design. In this chapter, expand your horizons and think about colored beading wire as a building block for sculpting your own unique shapes.

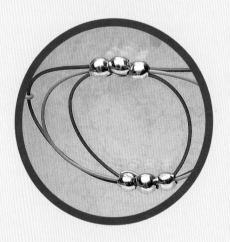

Believe

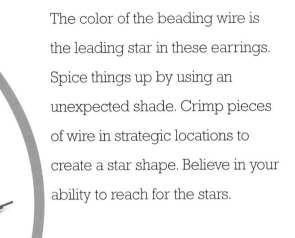

The color of the beading wire is the leading star in these earrings. Spice things up by using an unexpected shade. Crimp pieces of wire in strategic locations to create a star shape. Believe in your ability to reach for the stars.

materials

- Beading Wire (.019): 30 in. (76 cm) garnet
- **10** 8º turquoise seed beads
- **10** 2 x 2 mm sterling silver crimp tubes
- **10** 3 mm sterling silver crimp covers
- pair of sterling silver earring wires

tools

- chainnose pliers
- crimping pliers
- wire cutters

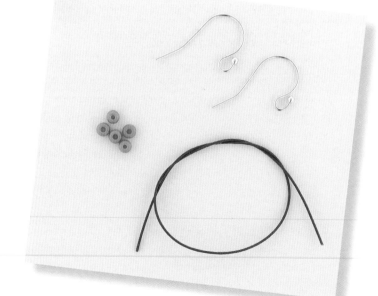

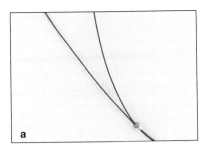

a

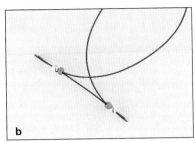

b

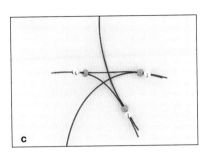

c

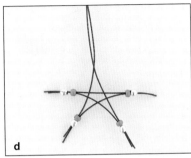

d

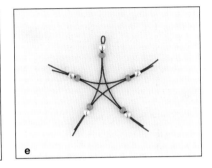

e

1 Cut the beading wire into 10 3-in. (7.6 cm) pieces.

2 On two 3-in. pieces of beading wire (wire 1 and wire 2), string a crimp tube. Crimp the crimp tube about ½ in. (1.3 cm) from the end of the wires. Cover the crimp with a crimp cover. Trim one short wire end ¼ in. (6 mm) from the crimp. Trim the other short wire end ⅜ in. (1 cm) from the crimp. Use both long ends of wire to string an 8º seed bead **[a]**.

3 Pick up a new 3-in. piece of wire (wire 3). On wire 2 and wire 3, string an 8º and a crimp tube. Place the crimp tube about 1⅛ in. (2.9 cm) from the previous crimp. Crimp the crimp tube and cover with a crimp cover. Trim one short wire end ¼ in. from the crimp. Trim the other short wire end ⅜ in. from the crimp **[b]**.

4 Pick up a new 3-in. piece of wire (wire 4). On wire 3 wire 4, string an 8º and a crimp tube. Place the crimp about 1⅛ in. from the previous crimp. Crimp and cover with a crimp cover. Trim one short wire end ¼ in. from the crimp. Trim the other short wire end ⅜ in. from the crimp **[c]**.

5 Pick up a new 3-in. piece of wire (wire 5). On wire 4 and wire 5, string an 8º and a crimp tube. Place the crimp tube about 1⅛ in. from the previous crimp. Crimp the crimp tube and cover with a crimp cover. Trim one short wire end ¼ in. from the crimp. Trim the other short wire end ⅜ in. from the crimp **[d]**.

6 On wire 1 and wire 5, string a seed bead and a crimp tube. Place the crimp tube about 1⅛ in. from the previous crimp. Pass one wire back through the crimp to make a loop. Crimp the crimp tube and cover with a crimp cover. Trim the extra wire flush to the crimp tube **[e]**.

7 Use chainnose pliers to attach the earring wire to the loop.

8 Make a second earring.

Don't stop with stars. Experiment with different wire lengths to make other creative shapes.

Mermaids

Texture is essential to jewelry design. Take advantage of the ability to use several sizes of crimps and crimping pliers on the same project. Crimp pieces of wire in strategic locations to create texture.

materials

- Beading Wire (.019):
  22 in. (56 cm) fluorite
- **20** 14º or 15º desert dust
  seed beads
- **20** 1 x 1 mm sterling silver
  crimp tubes
- **14** 2 x 2 mm sterling silver
  crimp tubes
- **14** 3 mm sterling silver crimp covers
- pair of sterling silver earring wires

tools

- chainnose pliers
- crimping pliers
- micro-crimping pliers
- wire cutters

Finished Size: 1⅝ in. (4.1 cm)

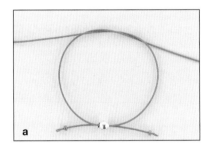

a

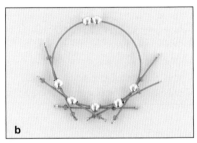

b

1 Cut the beading wire into two 6-in. (15 cm) and 10 1-in. (2.5 cm) pieces.

2 Use one 6-in. piece and one 1-in. piece of beading wire to string one 2 x 2 mm crimp tube to the center of both wires. Crimp the crimp tube. Cover the tube with a crimp cover.

3 On one end of the 1-in. wire, string a 14º seed bead and a 1 x 1 mm crimp tube. Place the crimp at the very end of the wire and crimp using micro-crimping pliers. Repeat on the other end of the 1-in. wire **[a]**.

4 On one end of the 6-in. wire and a 1-in. wire, string a 2 x 2 mm crimp tube. Place the crimp tube ¼ in. from the previous crimp tube on the 6-in. wire and at the center of the 1-in. wire. Crimp the crimp tube and cover with a crimp cover. Repeat Step 3.

5 Repeat Step 4 using the same end of the 6-in. wire.

6 Repeat Steps 4 and 5 using the other end of the 6-in. wire.

7 On one wire end, string two 2 x 2 mm crimp tubes. On the other end of the wire, string through the crimp tubes in the opposite direction. Adjust the wire ends to form a 25 mm diameter ring. Crimp the crimp tubes next to each other and cover each tube with a crimp cover **[b]**.

8 Use chainnose pliers to attach an earring wire between the two covered crimp tubes.

9 Make a second earring.

Am I Blue

Create your own favorite findings using colored beading wire. In these earrings, colored beading wire is strategically crimped to create a faux filigree shape.

materials

- Beading Wire (.019):
  18 in. (46 cm) tanzanite
- **12** 4 mm capri blue crystal bicones
- **24** 11º transparent amethyst
  seed beads
- **10** 2 x 2 mm sterling silver crimp tubes
- pair of sterling silver earring wires

tools

- chainnose pliers
- crimping pliers
- wire cutters

Finished Size: 1⅞ in. (4.8 cm)

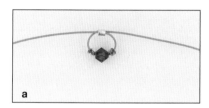

a

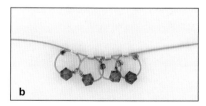

b

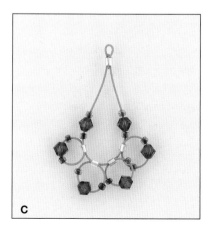

c

1 Cut a 9-in. (23 cm) length of beading wire. String a crimp tube, an 11º seed bead, a crystal, and a seed bead. String the wire through the crimp tube again to create a 7 mm loop. Adjust the loop so that it is about 1¼ in. (3.2 cm) from the end of the wire. Crimp the crimp tube **[a]**.

2 String a crimp tube, a seed bead, a crystal, and a seed bead. String the wire through the crimp again to create a 7 mm loop. Adjust the loop so that it is about ⅛ in. (3 mm) from the previous crimp. Crimp the crimp tube.

3 Repeat Step 2 twice for a total of four loops **[b]**.

4 String a seed bead, a crystal, and a seed bead on each wire end.

5 Over both wire ends, string a crimp tube. Pass one wire end back into the

crimp to create a small loop. Crimp the crimp tube. Trim the wire ends flush to the crimp tube **[c]**.

6 Use chainnose pliers to attach the earring wire to the loop.

7 Make a second earring.

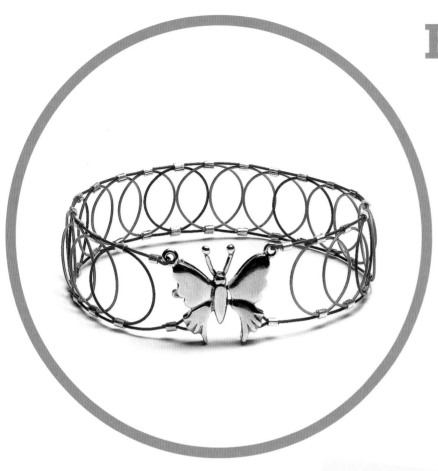

Elusive Butterfly

A simple repeated pattern can make a design that looks quite complex. In this bracelet, the repetition of an overlapping circle in three different colors lends a modern feel. An ornamental clasp, placed front and center, becomes part of the design.

materials

- Beading Wire (.019):
  17½ in. (43 cm) citrine
  31½ in. (80 cm) fluorite
  33½ in. (85.1 cm) red jasper
- **42** 2 x 2 mm sterling silver crimp tubes
- 2-strand sterling silver butterfly hook-and-eye clasp

tools

- crimping pliers
- wire cutters

Finished Size: 7 in. (18 cm)

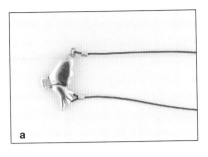

a

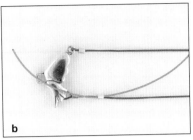

b

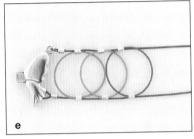

c

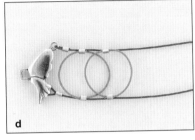

d

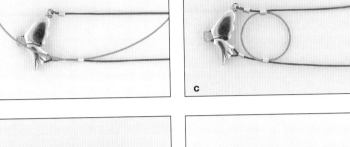

e

1 Cut an 8-in. (20 cm) length of red jasper beading wire. String a crimp tube and the top loop of the eye half of the clasp. Go back through the crimp tube and crimp.

2 Cut an 8-in. length of red jasper beading wire. String a crimp tube and the bottom loop of the eye half of the clasp. Go back through the crimp tube and crimp **[a]**.

3 Cut 3½ in. (8.9 cm) of citrine beading wire. String a crimp tube over the citrine wire and the red jasper wire from Step 2 **[b]**. Place the crimp tube ¼ in. (6 mm) from the previous crimp tube on the red jasper wire and at the center of the citrine wire, and crimp the crimp tube.

4 On the red jasper beading wire from Step 1, string a crimp tube. Pass the citrine wire ends through the crimp tube in opposite directions to create a 15 mm loop. Line this crimp up with the crimp from the previous step (¼ in. from the previous crimp tube on the red jasper wire) and crimp the crimp tube. Trim the citrine wire ends **[c]**.

5 Repeat Steps 3 and 4 using fluorite wire **[d]**. Repeat Steps 3 and 4 using red jasper wire. **[e]**. Repeat Steps 3 and 4 using fluorite wire.

6 Repeat Steps 3–5 three times. Repeat Steps 3 and 4. Repeat Steps 3 and 4 using fluorite wire. Repeat Steps 3 and 4 using red jasper wire.

7 Use the red jasper wire from Step 1 to string one crimp tube and the top loop of the hook half of the clasp. Adjust the crimp so it is ¼ in. from the previous crimp tube. Go back through the crimp tube and crimp.

8 Use the red jasper wire from Step 2 to string one crimp tube and the bottom loop of the hook half of the clasp. Adjust the crimp so that it is ¼ in. from the previous crimp tube. Go back through the crimp tube and crimp.

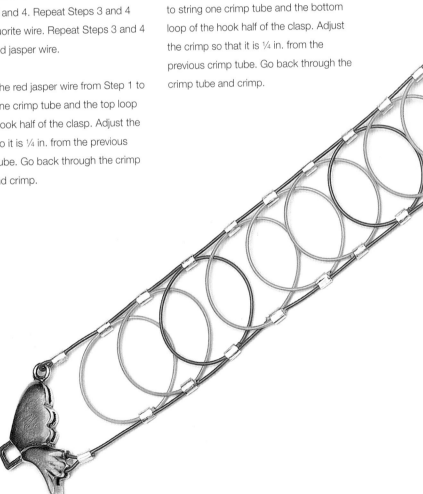

Fires of Eden

Create your own colorful focal point using colored beading wire. In this bracelet, the simple oval shape becomes an eye-catching and unique component.

materials

- Beading Wire (.019):
  16 in. (41 cm) citrine
  6 in. (15 cm) pink tourmaline
  6 in. spinel
- **2** 8 mm topaz crystal bicones
- **4** 6 mm topaz crystal bicones
- **4** 4 mm topaz crystal bicones
- **16** 11º opaque magenta seed beads
- **24** 15º opaque magenta seed beads
- **10** 2 x 2 mm sterling silver crimp tubes
- **6** 3 mm sterling silver crimp covers
- 20 mm sterling silver triangular toggle clasp

tools

- chainnose pliers
- crimping pliers
- wire cutters

Finished Size: 7 in. (18 cm)

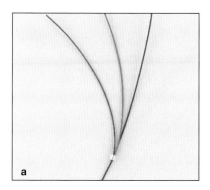

a

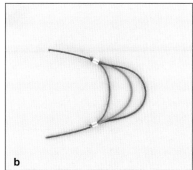

b

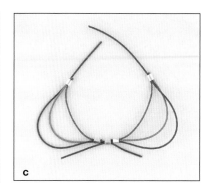

c

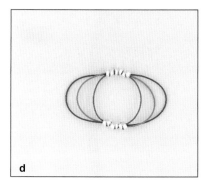

d

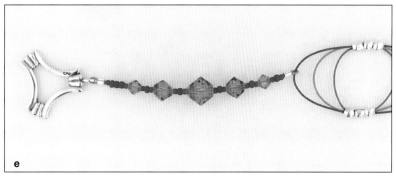

e

1 Cut a 3-in. (7.6 cm) length of each color of beading wire. String a crimp tube over all three wires. Place the crimp ½ in. (1.3 cm) from the wire ends, and crimp. Trim the short ends of the pink tourmaline and citrine wires; do not cut the spinel wire end **[a]**. String a crimp tube over the wires. Adjust the wires so that there is ⅞ in. (2.2 cm) of pink tourmaline wire between the crimps, 1¼ in. (3.2 cm) of citrine wire between the crimps, and 1¾ in. (4.4 cm) of spinel wire between the crimps. Crimp the crimp tube. Trim the pink tourmaline and citrine wire ends; do not cut the spinel wire end **[b]**. Set aside.

2 Repeat Step 1.

3 String a crimp tube on a spinel wire end from Step 1. With one spinel wire end from Step 2, string through the crimp in the opposite direction. Snug the wires tight so that all three crimps are aligned. Crimp the crimp tube **[c]** and trim the excess wire.

4 Repeat Step 3 using the other wire ends to create an oval **[d]**. Cover all the crimps with crimp covers.

5 Cut a 5-in. (13 cm) length of citrine wire. String a crimp tube and the spinel loop on one half of the oval. Go back through the tube and crimp.

6 String a 15º, an 11º, a 15º, and a 4 mm crystal. String a 15º, an 11º, a 15º, and a 6 mm crystal. String a 15º, an 11º, a 15º, and an 8 mm crystal. String a 15º, an 11º, a 15º, and, a 6 mm crystal. String a 15º, an 11º, a 15º, and a 4 mm crystal. String a 15º, three 11ºs, a 15º, a crimp tube, and one half of the toggle clasp. Go back through the tube and crimp **[e]**.

7 Repeat Steps 5 and 6 for the other half of the bracelet.

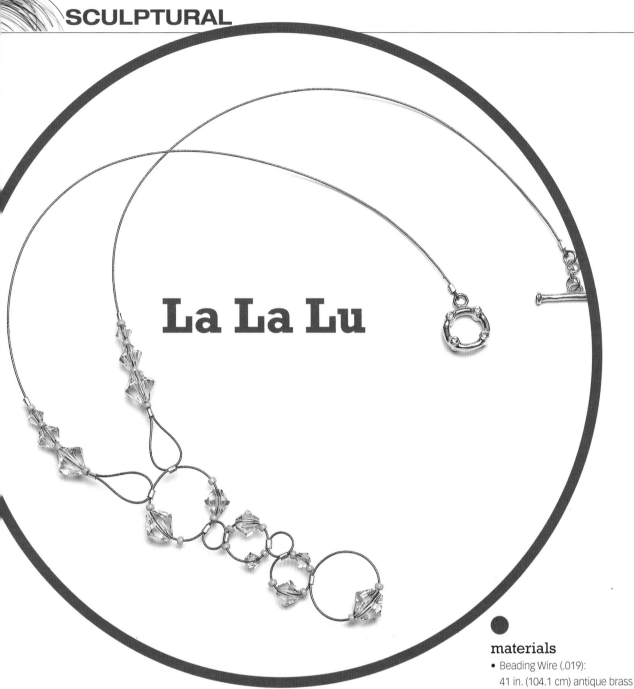

La La Lu

Play with size and shape, even in the same design. Not every part of a design has to be perfectly symmetrical. In this necklace, mix different sizes of loops made from colored beading wire.

materials

- Beading Wire (.019):
  41 in. (104.1 cm) antique brass
- **4** 8 mm light sapphire crystal bicones
- **5** 6 mm light sapphire crystal bicones
- **4** 4 mm light sapphire crystal bicones
- **22** 11º burnt sienna over opaque yellow-orange seed beads
- **13** 2 x 2 mm gold-filled crimp tubes
- 12 x 15 mm gold-filled with topaz crystals toggle clasp

tools

- crimping pliers
- wire cutters

Finished Size: 17¾ in. (45.1 cm)

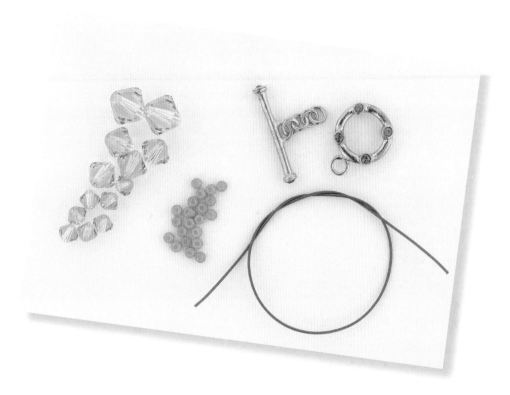

1 Cut a 30-in. (76 cm) length of beading wire. String and center a crimp tube, an 11º seed bead, an 8 mm crystal, and a seed bead. Go back through the crimp tube in the opposite direction to create a 15 mm loop. Crimp the crimp tube **[a]**.

2 On the left wire end, string a seed bead, a 6 mm crystal, a seed bead, and a crimp tube. On the right wire end, string a seed bead, a 4 mm crystal, and a seed bead. With the right wire, pass through the crimp in the opposite direction to create a 10 mm loop. Adjust the crimp so that it is off-center to the right, closer to the 4 mm crystal, and crimp the crimp tube **[b]**.

3 On the left wire end, string a crimp tube. Pass the right wire through the crimp in the opposite direction to create a 5 mm loop. Adjust the crimp so that it is off-center to the left, and crimp the crimp tube.

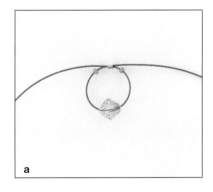

a

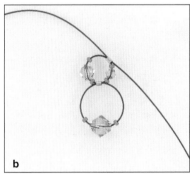

b

4 On the left wire end, string a seed bead, a 4 mm crystal, a seed bead, and a crimp tube. On the right wire end, string a seed bead, a 6 mm crystal, and a seed bead. String through the crimp in the opposite direction to create a 10 mm loop. Adjust the crimp so that it is off-center to the left, closer to the 4 mm crystal, and crimp the crimp tube.

5 On the left wire end, string a crimp tube. On the right wire end, string through the crimp in the opposite direction to create a 5 mm loop. Adjust the crimp so that it is off-center to the right, and crimp the crimp tube.

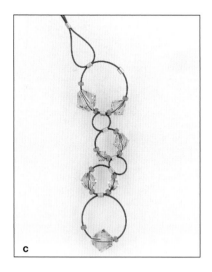

c

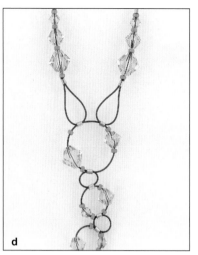

d

6 On the left wire end, string a seed bead, an 8 mm crystal and a seed bead. On the right wire end, string a seed bead, a 6 mm crystal, a seed bead, and two crimp tubes. Use the left wire to string through the closest crimp in the opposite direction to create a 15 mm loop. Adjust the crimp so it is off-center to the left, closer to the 8 mm crystal, and then crimp the crimp tube. Leave the other crimp tube uncrimped.

7 Over both wire ends, string a crimp tube to create a teardrop shape. Adjust the crimp so that the teardrop is about 15 mm from top to bottom and 7 mm from side to side at the widest part **[c]**. Crimp the crimp tube and trim one of the two wire ends.

8 On the remaining wire end, string a seed bead, an 8 mm crystal, a seed bead, a 6 mm crystal, a seed bead, a 4 mm crystal, a seed bead, and a crimp tube. Snug the beads to the previous crimp tube, and crimp the crimp tube.

9 String a crimp tube and one half of the clasp. Go back through the crimp tube and crimp.

10 Cut 11 in. (28 cm) of beading wire and string a crimp tube. Pass through the open crimp tube from Step 6. Go back through the crimp tube just strung to create a teardrop shape. Adjust the crimp so the teardrop is about 15 mm from top to bottom and 7 mm from side to side at the widest part. Crimp the crimp tube and trim one of the two wire ends. Crimp the open crimp tube from Step 6 **[d]**.

11 Repeat Step 8 and 9 to finish the necklace.

Make a matching bracelet by extending the pattern in the pendant for a few more inches and adding a clasp.

Chapter 5

BRAIDING AND WEAVING

Braided and woven designs showcase the versatility of colored beading wire. In this chapter, you'll find a new twist on age-old traditions. Simple braided beading wire is a beautiful addition to any design. Braid several colors together to create an interesting color combination, weave in and out of craft wire, or use seed beads to create a continuous woven pattern.

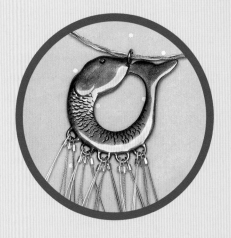

Holding Out for Love

Nine strands of wire, in colors that perfectly match the beads and findings, are braided together to form the back of this bright and cheerful necklace. Using mostly silver wire with only one strand each of purple amethyst, citrine, and red jasper adds the perfect amount of color to this textural technique.

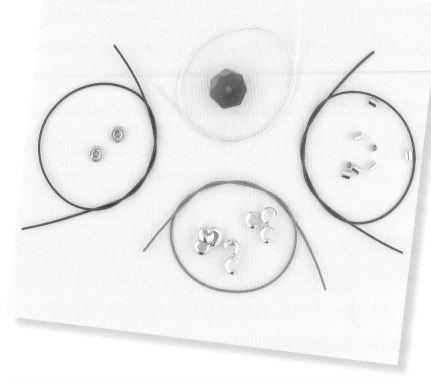

materials

- Beading Wire (.019):
  108 in. (2.8 m) .925 sterling silver
  18 in. (46 cm) red jasper
  18 in. purple amethyst
  18 in. citrine
- 19 x 16 mm yellow with red-and-purple flowers lampworked rondelle
- 16 x 12 mm putty with orange/red/ purple/yellow flowers lampworked rondelle
- 10 x 8 mm purple with orange dots lampworked rondelle
- **2** 16 mm purple ceramic botanical coins
- **6** 8 x 6 mm yellow-and-orange AB Czech fire-polished rondelles
- **18** 4 mm silver flat spacers
- **4** 9 x 2 mm sterling silver spiral bead caps
- **4** 10 x 4 mm sterling silver flower bead caps
- 31 in. (79 cm) 22-gauge non-tarnish silver craft wire
- **10** 2 x 2 mm sterling silver crimp tubes
- **10** 3 mm sterling silver crimp covers
- 25 mm sterling silver flower button/ toggle clasp

tools

- roundnose pliers
- chainnose pliers
- crimping pliers
- wire cutters

Finished size: 21¾ in. (55.2 cm)

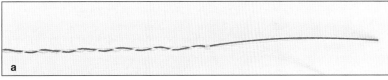

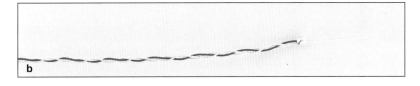

1 Cut the sterling silver beading wire into six 18-in. (46 cm) lengths.

2 On two sterling silver and the red wires, string a crimp tube. Place the crimp tube 2 in. (5 cm) from the wire ends, and crimp. Braid the three wires together until there is 2 in. remaining on each wire **[a]**. String a crimp tube over all three wires. Place the crimp tube at the end of the braid, and crimp. Trim one sterling silver wire and the red wire from both ends of the braid—do not cut the remaining sterling silver wire. Cover each crimp with a crimp cover. Set aside **[b]**.

3 Repeat Step 2 with two sterling silver wire lengths and the purple wire.

4 Repeat Step 2 with two sterling silver wire lengths and the citrine wire.

5 String a crimp tube over all three braids from Steps 2–4 **[c]**. Snug the crimp as close as possible to the crimp covers and crimp **[d]**. Trim two wire ends. Cover the crimp tube with a crimp cover **[e]**. Use the remaining wire to string a silver spacer, a fire-polished rondelle, a silver spacer, and a crimp. Go back through the crimp, leaving a small loop of wire, and crimp. Cover with a crimp cover **[f]**.

6 Braid the three braided strands together. Repeat Step 5 at the other end of the braid.

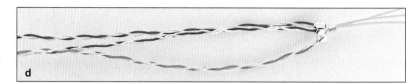

For the remainder of the necklace, you will be making a series of connected wrapped-loop links.

Link 1 (connects to loop at one end of braid): Use 3 in. of craft wire. Make a wrapped loop through the beading wire loop made in Step 5. String a silver spacer, a fire-polished rondelle, and a spacer. Finish with a wire-wrapped loop **[g]**.

Link 2: Use 3 in. of craft wire. Make a wrapped loop through link 1. String a silver spacer, the 10 x 8 mm lampworked rondelle, and a spacer. Finish with a wire-wrapped loop.

Link 3: Use 3 in. of craft wire. Make a wrapped loop through link 2. String a silver spacer, a fire-polished rondelle, and a spacer. Finish with a wire-wrapped loop through the button part of the clasp.

Link 4: Use 3 in. of craft wire. Make a wrapped loop through the loop at the other end of the braid. String a silver spacer, a fire-polished rondelle, and a spacer. Finish with a wire-wrapped loop.

Link 5: Use 4 in. of craft wire. Make a wrapped loop through link 4. String a silver spacer, a spiral bead cap, the 16 x 12 mm lampworked rondelle, a spiral bead cap, and a spacer. Finish with a wire-wrapped loop.

Link 6: Use 4 in. of craft wire. Make a wrapped loop through link 5. String a flower bead cap (narrow end first), a ceramic coin, and a flower bead cap (wide end first). Finish with a wire-wrapped loop.

Link 7: Use 4 in. of craft wire. Make a wrapped loop through link 6. String a silver spacer, a spiral bead cap, the 19 x 16 mm lampworked rondelle, a spiral bead cap, and a spacer. Finish with a wire-wrapped loop.

Link 8: Use 4 in. of craft wire. Make a wrapped loop through link 7. String a flower bead cap (narrow end first), a ceramic coin, and a flower bead cap (wide end first). Finish with a wire-wrapped loop.

Link 9 (connects to link 8 and the flower/ring half of the clasp): Use 3 in. of craft wire. Make a wrapped loop through link 8. String a silver spacer, a fire-polished rondelle, and a silver spacer. Finish with a wire-wrapped loop connecting the ring half of the clasp.

Malibu

In this set of bangles, three wire colors are blended together in eight different braids that all feature seed beads or copper beads and charms. When worn together, these simple bracelets make a powerful fashion statement.

materials

- Beading Wire (.019):
  140 in. (3.6 m) chrysoprase
  112 in. (2.9 m) blue topaz
  84 in. (2.2 m) yellow lemon quartz
- Charms:
  10 x 24 mm antique copper sea horse
  8 x 23 mm antique copper spindle shell
  18 x 20 mm antique copper sea star
- 13 mm antique copper large shell bead
- **7** 10 x 6 mm antique copper large-hole divot beads

- **25** 11º transparent light yellow AB seed beads
- **25** 11º shimmering sky blue-lined seed beads
- **26** 11º metallic light peridot-lined citrine seed beads
- **8** 3 x 3 mm sterling silver crimp tubes
- 10 ft. (3.1 m) 28-gauge bare copper craft wire

tools

- chainnose pliers
- mighty crimping pliers
- wire cutters
- pre-fabricated bangle bracelet or bracelet mandrel
- bead stoppers

Finished Size:
2¾ in. (7 cm) (diameter)

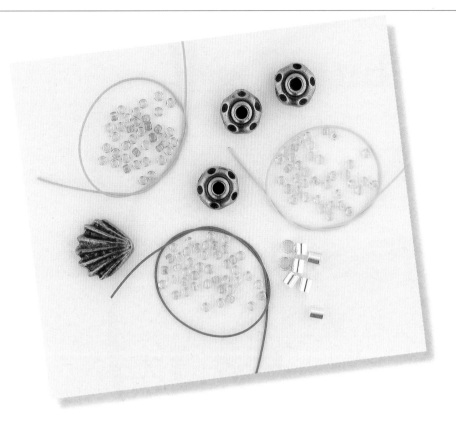

Cut the chrysoprase beading wire into 10 14-in. (36 cm) pieces. Cut the blue topaz beading wire into eight 14-in. pieces. Cut the yellow lemon quartz beading wire into six 14-in. pieces.

Bangle 1

1 Attach a bead stopper to the end of three pieces of chrysoprase wire. String a crimp tube over all the wires. Braid the wires for 8-in. (20 cm). String seven large-hole divot beads over the braid.

2 Pass all three wire ends through the crimp tube again. Use the pre-fabricated bangle or the mandrel as a guide, adjust the wires to form a ring, and crimp. Remove the bead stopper and trim the wire ends. Use 14 in. of 28-gauge bare copper wire to wrap around the crimp tube until it is covered with wire. Use chainnose pliers to tuck the wire ends into the wrap **[a]**.

Bangle 2

Gather a piece of chrysoprase wire, a piece of blue topaz wire, and a piece of yellow lemon quartz wire together and attach a bead stopper to the end. String a crimp tube over all three wires. Braid the wires together for 3½ in. (8.9 cm). String the large shell bead onto the yellow lemon quartz wire. Push the bead to the braid. Continue to braid the wires together for 3¾ in. (9.5 cm). Finish the bangle as in Step 2 of Bangle 1 **[b]**.

Bangle 3

Attach a bead stopper to the end of three pieces of blue topaz wire. String a crimp tube over all three wires. Braid the wires together for 2 in. (5 cm). String the spindle shell charm on one wire. Push the charm to the braid. Continue to braid the wires together for 6 in. (15 cm). Finish the bangle as in Step 2 of Bangle 1 **[c]**.

Bangle 4

Gather two pieces of chrysoprase wire and one piece of blue topaz wire. Attach a bead stopper to one end. String a crimp tube over all three wires. Braid the wires together for 3¾ in. (9.5 cm). String the sea horse charm onto the blue wire. Push the charm to the braid. Continue to braid the wires together for 4 in. (10 cm). Finish the bangle as in Step 2 of Bangle 1 **[d]**.

Bangle 5

Gather two pieces of yellow lemon quartz wire and one piece of chrysoprase wire. Attach a bead stopper to one end. String a crimp tube over all the wires. Braid the wires together for ¾ in. (1.9 cm). String a sea star charm on one strand of yellow wire. Push the charm up to the braid. Continue to braid the wires together for 7¼ in. (18.4 cm). Finish the bangle as in Step 2 of Bangle 1 **[e]**.

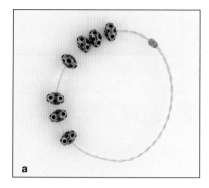

a

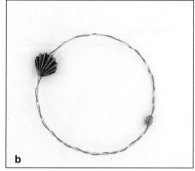

b

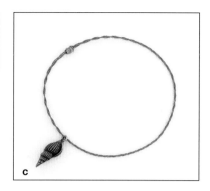

c

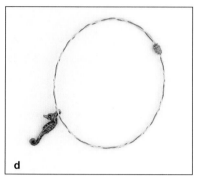

d

e

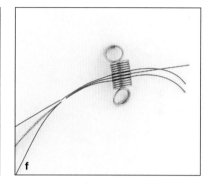

f

Bangle 6

Attach a bead stopper to the end of three pieces of blue topaz beading wire. String 25 shimmering sky blue-lined seed beads on the middle wire **[f]**. Place a bead stopper on this wire end. Begin braiding the wires together. Every time the original middle wire passes to the middle of the braid, slide a seed bead up into the braid **[g]**. Continue this for 8 in. (20 cm). Finish the bangle as in Step 2 of Bangle 1 **[h]**.

Bangle 7

Follow the directions for Bangle 6 using yellow lemon quartz wire and transparent light yellow AB seed beads.

Bangle 8

Follow the directions for Bangle 6 using chrysoprase wire and metallic light peridot-lined citrine seed beads **[i]**.

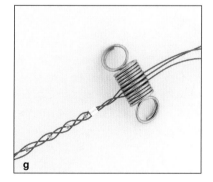

g

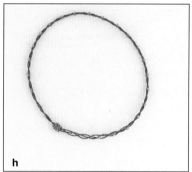

h

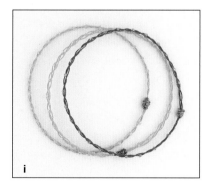

i

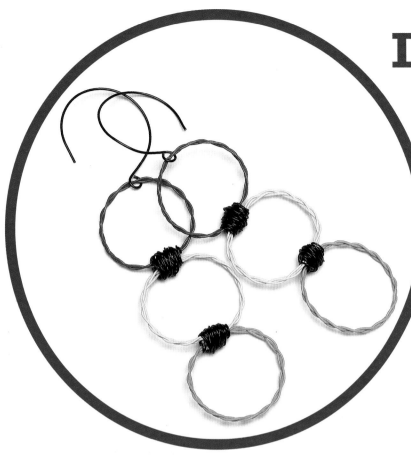

Dead Ringer for Love

Braided wire rings in bright pops of color are all you need for fun earrings. With black craft wire covering the crimp tubes while connecting the rings, colored beading wire becomes the focal point of the entire design.

materials
- Beading Wire (.019):
  36 in. (.9 m) fluorite
  36 in. bone
  36 in. red coral
- 6 3 x 3 mm sterling silver crimp tubes
- 6 in. (15 cm) 20-gauge black craft wire
- 64 in. (1.6 m) 26-gauge black craft wire

tools
- chainnose pliers
- roundnose pliers
- mighty crimping pliers
- wire cutters
- WigJig® with ¾ in. premium peg
- bead stoppers

Finished Size: 3¾ in. (9.5 cm)

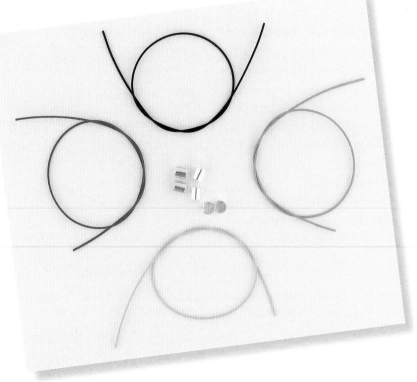

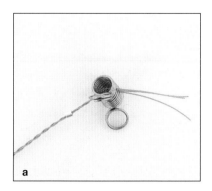

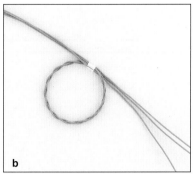

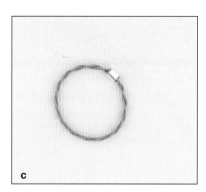

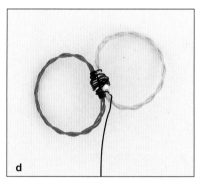

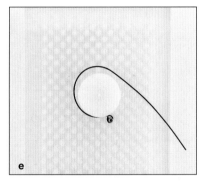

1 Cut each color of beading wire into six 6-in. (15 cm) pieces.

2 Place a bead stopper on the ends of three pieces of fluorite beading wire. String a crimp tube over all three wires. Braid the wires together for 3 in. (7.6 cm) **[a]**. Pass all three wire ends through the crimp again, forming a 24–25 mm diameter ring. Remove the bead stopper and crimp **[b]**. Trim all wire ends **[c]**.

3 Repeat Step 2 with the remaining wire to form a second fluorite ring, two bone rings, and two red coral rings. Set aside.

4 Use your non-dominant hand to hold a bone braided ring and a red coral braided ring together so that their crimp tubes are aligned. Use 16 in. (41 cm) of 26-gauge craft wire to wrap around both rings, covering the crimp tubes **[d]**. Use chainnose pliers to tuck the wire ends into the wraps.

5 Hold a fluorite ring next to the bone ring used in Step 4, so that the crimp tube of the fluorite aligns opposite the crimp tube of the bone ring. Use 16 in. of 26-gauge craft wire to wrap around both rings, covering the crimp tube. Use chainnose pliers to tuck the wire ends into the wraps. Set aside.

6 Repeat Steps 4 and 5 to make a second earring.

7 Place a regular WigJig peg and the premium peg into the WigJig as in photo **[e]**. Use roundnose pliers to form a loop at one end of 3 in. of 22-gauge craft wire, making sure the loop is just large enough to fit over the regular peg. Place the loop over the peg, making sure the end of the wire is facing the premium peg. Turn the WigJig to wrap the wire around the premium peg one complete turn to form a round earring wire **[e]**. Gently remove the earring wire from the WigJig and trim the wire end so that there is about ½ in. (1.3 cm) of open space between the loop and the wire end. Repeat this entire step to form a second earring wire.

8 Attach an earring wire as desired to each component.

Bang Bang

Mix it up! In this bracelet, you will work with
both colored beading wire and craft wire.
Create shapes from craft wire and then weave
the colored beading wire through to make this
one-of-a-kind design.

materials

- Beading Wire (.019):
  20 in. (51 cm) amethyst
  20 in. chrysoprase
  20 in. turquoise
- 4 ft. (1.3 m) 20-gauge non-tarnish
  silver craft wire
- 4 3 x 3 mm sterling silver crimp tubes
- 12 x 17 mm 2-strand sterling silver
  magnetic clasp

tools

- roundnose pliers
- mighty crimping pliers
- nylon jaw pliers
- wire cutters
- WigJig®
- nylon hammer
- Anvil or bench block

Finished Size: 7 in. (18 cm)

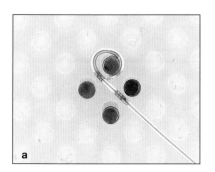

a

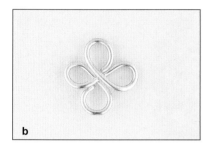

b

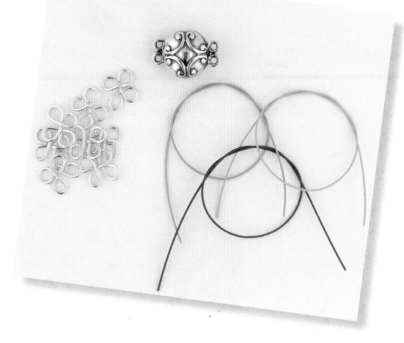

c

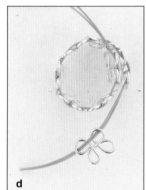

d

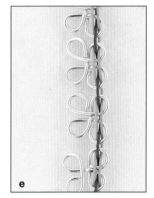

e

f

1 Insert four pegs into the WigJig in a diamond formation.

2 Cut 16 3-in. (7.6 cm) lengths of craft wire. Use roundnose pliers to form a loop on one end of a piece of wire. Slide the loop onto the WigJig. Turn the WigJig to wrap the wire around all four pegs, creating a double figure-8 link. Repeat 15 times for a total of 16 links. Use the nylon hammer and anvil or bench block to work-harden all links. Set aside **[a, b]**.

3 Cut 10 in. (25 cm) of chrysoprase and turquoise beading wire. Hold the wires together and string the first loop of a link, leaving 2-in. (5 cm) tail. Pass the wires down through the next loop of the link. *String the first loop of a link. Pass down through the next loop of the link. Repeat from * fourteen times, keeping in mind that the woven piece will curl as you add links **[c, d]**.

4 Use 10 in. of amethyst wire to weave through the links in the opposite direction as the previous wires, through the middle of each link between the two previous wires **[e]**.

5 Repeat Steps 3 and 4 using the remaining two loops of each link.

6 Use one end of all three wires used in Steps 3 and 4 to string a crimp tube and one loop of one half of the clasp. Go back through the tube and crimp. Repeat using one end of all three wires used in Step 5. Repeat the entire step for the other end of the bracelet **[f]**.

Homeward Bound

For this bracelet, weave the colored beading wire through beads to create a pattern. The colored beading wire is perfect for making circles and loops.

materials
- Beading Wire (.019): 66 in. (1.7 m) fluorite
- **137** 8º metallic dark eggplant seed beads
- **10** 4 mm sterling silver jump rings
- **12** 2 x 2 mm sterling silver crimp tubes
- **12** 3 mm sterling silver crimp covers
- 31 x 11 mm 3-strand sterling silver slide clasp

tools
- chainnose pliers
- crimping pliers
- wire cutters

Finished Size: 7 in. (18 cm)

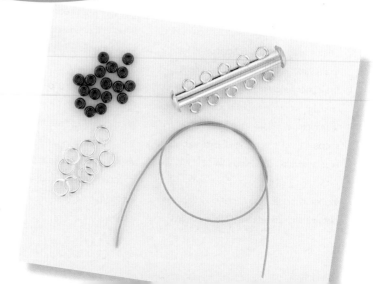

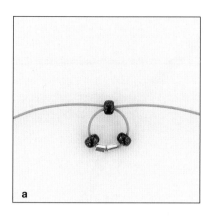

a

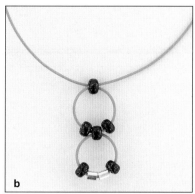

b

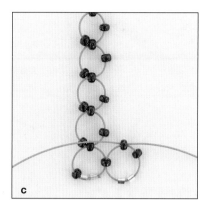

c

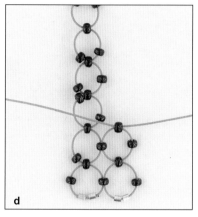

d

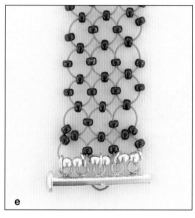

e

6 Repeat Step 5 17 times for a total of 19 loops. Use one wire end to string through the last seed bead of the band. String a crimp tube. Use the other wire end to string a seed bead and a crimp tube. Pass back through both crimp tubes with the other wire in the opposite direction. Pull to form a 7 mm ring. Crimp all four crimp tubes.

7 Repeat Steps 4–6 for the third row of loops.

8 Cover each crimp tube with a crimp cover.

9 Use a jump ring to attach the middle ring on one end of the bracelet to the center loop of one half of the clasp, placing the jump ring between the two crimp covers. *Use a jump ring to attach the right ring to the loop right of center on the same half of the clasp, placing the jump ring to the left of the left crimp cover. Use a jump ring to attach the right ring to the far right loop of the same half of the clasp, placing the jump ring to the right of the right crimp cover. Repeat from * for the left of center. Repeat the entire step for the other end of the bracelet, using the other half of the clasp **[e]**.

1 Cut three 22-in. (56 cm) pieces of beading wire. Center a seed bead, two crimp tubes, and a seed bead on a wire. String a seed bead on one end and pass the other end through the bead in the opposite direction. Adjust the wires to form a ring about 7 mm in diameter **[a]**.

2 String two seed beads on one end. String a seed bead on the other end, then pass this wire through the second seed bead strung at the beginning of this step in the opposite direction **[b]**.

3 Repeat Step 2 17 times for a total of 19 loops. On each wire, string a seed bead and a crimp tube. Using the opposite wire end, pass back through both crimp tubes in the opposite direction to form a 7 mm ring. Crimp all four crimp tubes.

4 Use a 22-in. piece of beading wire to string through the first seed bead at the bottom right of the band formed in Steps 1–3. Use the other end of the wire to string two crimp tubes and a seed bead. Center the beads and crimps on the wire. String a seed bead on one wire. With the other wire, pass back through the seed bead in the opposite direction. Adjust the wires to form a ring about 7 mm in diameter to start the second row of loops **[c]**.

5 With one wire end, string through the next seed bead of the band. On the other end of the wire, string two seed beads. With the opposite wire, pass back through the second seed bead in the opposite direction. Adjust the wires to form a ring about 7 mm **[d]**.

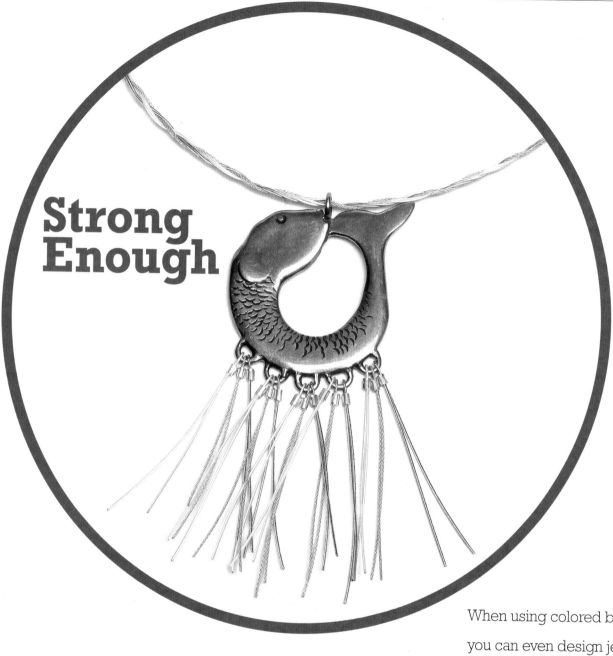

Strong Enough

When using colored beading wire, you can even design jewelry with no beads at all. In this design, several metallic beading wires create an elegant look.

materials

- Beading Wire (.019):
  59 in. (1.5 m) 24k gold
  59 in. 925 sterling silver
  59 in. champagne
- 36 x 40 bronze fish pendant
- **2** 3 x 3 mm sterling silver crimp tubes
- **15** 2 x 2 mm sterling silver crimp tubes
- 17 x 20 mm bronze toggle clasp

tools

- crimping pliers
- mighty crimping pliers
- wire cutters
- bead stopper

Finished Size: 17½ in. (44.5 cm)

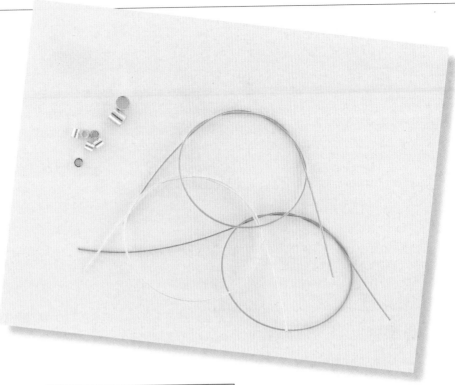

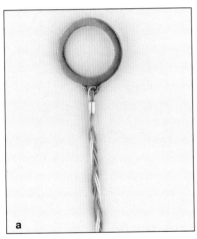

a

b

4 Over all six 22-in. wires, string a 3 x 3 mm crimp tube and the other clasp half. Go back through the tube and slide the tube so that it is right next to the bead stopper. Remove the bead stopper and adjust the tube, if necessary. Crimp the tube and trim the tail wires **[a]**.

5 Use one 3-in. piece of gold beading wire to string one loop at the bottom of the pendant to the center of the wire. Use both wire ends to string one 2 x 2 mm crimp tube. Place the tube just below the pendant loop, and crimp. Repeat with sterling silver beading wire and champagne wire on the same pendant loop **[b]**.

6 Repeat Step 5 four times, attaching three wires to each pendant loop.

1 Cut each color of wire into two 22-in. (56 cm) and five 3-in. (7.6 cm) pieces. Set the 3-in. wires aside.

2 Over all six 22-in. (56 cm) wires, string a 3 x 3 mm crimp tube and a clasp half. Go back through the tube and crimp.

3 Divide the wire by color into three groups of two strands each. Braid the wires for about 16¼ in. (41.3 cm). String the pendant. Place a bead stopper on wires at the end of the braid to keep them from unraveling.

Shopping for beads is one of our favorite things to do. We know how frustrating it can be when you can't find what you're looking for! Here are some sources for unique beads and findings we used in this book:

Mirror Image, p. 24
Black pewter earring wires, crimps, and spacers, Tierra Cast.

Dark Lady, p. 26
Antique gold toggle clasp, Tierra Cast.
SWAROVSKI ELEMENTS crystals and crystal pearls.

Rain Rain, p. 28
Clasp, Shiana.

Emotional Fire, p. 32
Lampwork bead, Nancy Pilgrim, Fantasy Beads.

Magic in the Air, p. 36
Antique silver pewter beads, spacers, and clasp, Tierra Cast.

How Pretty the Moon, p. 39
Antique gold pewter spacers and earring wires, Tierra Cast.
SWAROVSKI ELEMENTS crystal pearls.

Holy Smoke, p. 41
SWAROVSKI ELEMENTS crystal pearls.
Antique silver pewter beads, Tierra Cast.

Dream Baby, p. 44
Pewter pendant, Green Girl Studios.

Burlesque, p. 52
Natural brass beads, cones, and toggle clasp, Vintaj Natural Brass Company.

Moonstruck, p. 54
Enameled pendant, Bronwen Heilman.

Heart of Stone, p. 57
Cones, Soft Flex Company or Pacific Silverworks.

Silkwood, p. 59
Hammered Thai silver cones and toggle clasp, Bead Cache.

Caesar's Palace, p. 61
Clasp, Soft Flex Company.

Am I Blue, p. 67
SWAROVSKI ELEMENTS crystals.

Elusive Butterfly, p. 68
Clasp, Soft Flex Company.

Holding Out for Love, p. 76
Lampwork beads, Dyed in the Fire Designs.
Ceramic beads, Earthenwood Studio.
Spacers, Tierra Cast.
Sterling silver bead caps and clasp, Springall Adventures.

Malibu, p. 79
Antique copper pewter charms and beads, Tierra Cast.

Strong Enough, p. 88
Clasp and pendant, Saki silver.

There are many places to shop for beads. Check your local bead shop first—it's a great resource. Here are some of our other favorites:

Artbeads.com
866-715-BEAD (2323)
support@artbeads.com
artbeads.com

Bead Cache
(970) 224-4322
bead-cache.com

Beyond Beadery
800-840-5548
info@beyondbeadery.com
beyondbeadery.com

Bronwen Heilman
Ghostcow Glassworks
bronwenheilman.com

Dyed in the Fire Designs
Patti Cahill
plcahill@madison.main.nc.us
patticahill.etsy.com

Earthenwood Studio
Melanie Brooks
earthenwood@gmail.com
earthenwoodstudio.com

Fantasy Beads
Nancy Pilgrim
480-892-4330
info@nancypilgrim.com
nancypilgrim.com

Fusionbeads.com
888-781-3559
fusionbeads.com

Green Girl Studios
877-GGSTUDIOS
greengirlstudios@gmail.com
greengirlstudios.com

Pacific Silverworks
805-641-1394
sales@pacificsilverworks.com
pacificsilverworks.com

Raven's Journey
sales@theravenstore.com
theravenstore.com

Saki
513-221-5480
liz@sakisilver.com
sakisilver.com

Shiana
shiana.com

Soft Flex® Company
1-866-925-FLEX
info@softflexcompany.com
softflexcompany.com

Springall Adventures
Pam Springall
505-757-6520
springadv@cybermesa.com

Tierra Cast
800-222-9939
tierracast.com

Vintaj Natural Brass Co.
info@vintaj.com
vintaj.com

Photography Credit
Step-by-step photography by Brian Clark.

We were given help by many along the way. We are grateful to the entire Soft Flex® Company team for their assistance and patience in creating this book, with extra special thanks to Brian Clark for his amazing help with photos. Thank you to Lorelei Eurto for inspiring us with her fun and stylish sense of design; Margie Deeb for sharing her color expertise; Fusion Beads and Tierra Cast for help with beads and findings; Linda Franzblau for planting the idea of this book in our heads; Jean Campbell for her infinite wisdom and friendship; and Karin Van Voorhees for believing in this project and letting us freely explore our boundaries in the creative process.

This book would not exist without the love and support of those closest to me. I especially want to thank my best friend, Erin, for her many years of friendship and fabulous sense of style; my mom, Denise, for always believing in me; and my new husband, Joshua, for his extraordinary and unconditional love and support.

Sara Hardin Oehler is a well-known jewelry designer residing in sunny Phoenix, Ariz. She has designed jewelry and written for numerous publications including: *BeadStyle*, *Bead&Button*, *Stringing*, *Jewelry in Fashion Trends*, *Simply Beads*, *The Flow*, and *Today's Creative Home Arts*. As "Ask Sara" of Soft Flex® Company, she has had the opportunity to have her work featured in advertisements, signs, fliers, postcards, and other marketing materials. Sara has attended, showed her designs, demonstrated and taught at hundreds of bead shows in her 13-year career. Currently, Sara is launching her own jewelry design business, *Sara O Jewelry*.

Sara's *Show Your Colors* projects are: Melody, p. 31, Emotional Fire, p. 32, Angels Running, p. 34, Dream Baby, p. 44, Carnival, p. 45, Fire and Rain, p. 47, Believe, p. 64, Mermaids, p. 66, Am I Blue, p. 67, Elusive Butterfly, p. 68, Fires of Eden, p. 70, La La Lu, p. 72, Bang Bang, p. 84, Homeward Bound, p. 86, and Strong Enough, p. 88.

As always, I'm thankful for the ever-present love and encouragement of all my family and friends. Special appreciation goes to my mom, Gail, and my grandma, Jane, for their support and rave reviews upon seeing the finished projects, and for always being willing models for my jewelry.

Jamie Hogsett is a bead lover, jewelry designer, beading instructor, freelance editor, and the Education Coordinator for Soft Flex® Company. She is the author of *Stringing Style* and co-author, with Marlene Blessing, of *Create Jewelry: Pearls*, *Create Jewelry: Crystals*, *Create Jewelry: Stones*, and *Create Jewelry: Glass*.

Jamie's work has been published numerous times in *BeadStyle, Stringing,* and *Beadwork* magazines, as well as in *Beadwork Creates Beaded Rings*, *Beadwork Creates Beaded Bags*, *Beadwork Creates Beaded Earrings,* and other books and magazines.

Jamie's *Show Your Colors* Projects are: Mirror Image, p. 24, Dark Lady, p. 26, Rain Rain, p. 28, Melody, p. 31, Magic in the Air, p. 36, How Pretty the Moon, p. 39, Holy Smoke, p. 41, Long and Winding Road, p. 50, Burlesque, p. 52, Moonstruck, p. 54, Heart of Stone, p. 57, Silkwood, p. 59, Caesar's Palace, p. 61, Holding Out for Love, p. 76, Malibu, p. 79, and Dead Ringer for Love, p. 82.

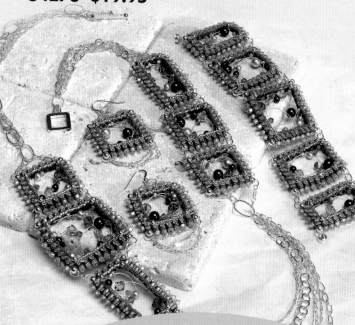